W9-AYF-685

THE EVOLUTION
OF AFRICA'S MAJOR NATIONS

Africa
Facts and Figures

THE EVOLUTION
OF AFRICA'S MAJOR NATIONS

Africa
Facts and Figures

William Mark Habeeb

Mason Crest
Philadelphia

Mason Crest
370 Reed Road
Broomall, PA 19008
www.masoncrest.com

CPSIA Compliance Information: Batch #EAMN2013-1. For further information,
contact Mason Crest at 1-866-MCP-Book.

First printing

1 3 5 7 9 8 6 4 2

Library of Congress Cataloging-in-Publication Data

Habeeb, William Mark, 1955-
  Africa : facts and figures / William Mark Habeeb.
      p. cm. — (The evolution of Africa's major nations.)
  Includes bibliographical references and index.
  ISBN 978-1-4222-2176-1 (hardcover)
  ISBN 978-1-4222-2204-1 (pbk.)
  ISBN 978-1-4222-9417-8 (ebook)
  1. Africa—Juvenile literature. I. Title. II. Series: Evolution of Africa's major nations.
  DT5.H23 2011
  960—dc22
                            2010048000

Africa: Facts and Figures
The African Union
Algeria
Angola
Botswana
Burundi
Cameroon
Democratic Republic
   of the Congo

Egypt
Ethiopia
Ghana
Ivory Coast
Kenya
Liberia
Libya
Morocco
Mozambique

Nigeria
Rwanda
Senegal
Sierra Leone
South Africa
Sudan and Southern Sudan
Tanzania
Uganda
Zimbabwe

Table of Contents

Africa: Progress, Problems, and Promise

Robert I. Rotberg

Africa is the cradle of humankind, but for millennia it was off the familiar, beaten path of global commerce and discovery. Its many peoples therefore developed largely apart from the diffusion of modern knowledge and the spread of technological innovation until the 17th through 19th centuries. With the coming to Africa of the book, the wheel, the hoe, and the modern rifle and cannon, foreigners also brought the vastly destructive transatlantic slave trade, oppression, discrimination, and onerous colonial rule. Emerging from that crucible of European rule, Africans created nationalistic movements and then claimed their numerous national independences in the 1960s. The result is the world's largest continental assembly of new countries.

There are 53 members of the African Union, a regional political grouping, and 48 of those nations lie south of the Sahara. Fifteen of them, including mighty Ethiopia, are landlocked, making international trade and economic growth that much more arduous and expensive. Access to navigable rivers is limited, natural harbors are few, soils are poor and thin, several countries largely consist of miles and miles of sand, and tropical diseases have sapped the strength and productivity of innumerable millions. Being landlocked, having few resources (although countries along Africa's west coast have tapped into deep offshore petroleum and gas reservoirs), and being beset by malaria, tuberculosis, schistosomiasis, AIDS, and many other maladies has kept much of Africa poor for centuries.

Thirty-two of the world's poorest 44 countries are African. Hunger is common. So is rapid deforestation and desertification. Unemployment rates are often over 50 percent, for jobs are few—even in agriculture. Where Africa once

An elephant wades into a river in the Hwange National Park, Zimbabwe.

was a land of small villages and a few large cities, with almost everyone engaged in growing grain or root crops or grazing cattle, camels, sheep, and goats, today more than half of all the more than 1 billion Africans, especially those who live south of the Sahara, reside in towns and cities. Traditional agriculture hardly pays, and a number of countries in Africa—particularly the smaller and more fragile ones—can no longer feed themselves.

There is not one Africa, for the continent is full of contradictions and variety. Of the 750 million people living south of the Sahara, at least 150 million live in Nigeria, 85 million in Ethiopia, 68 million in the Democratic Republic of the Congo, and 49 million in South Africa. By contrast, tiny Djibouti and Equatorial Guinea have fewer than 1 million people each, and prosperous Botswana and Namibia each are under 2.2 million in population. Within some countries, even medium-sized ones like Zambia (12 million), there are a plethora of distinct ethnic groups speaking separate languages. Zambia, typical with

Two men paddle a small boat on Lake Victoria, the second-largest freshwater lake in the world.

its multitude of competing entities, has 70 such peoples, roughly broken down into four language and cultural zones. Three of those languages jostle with English for primacy.

Given the kaleidoscopic quality of African culture and deep-grained poverty, it is no wonder that Africa has developed economically and politically less rapidly than other regions. Since independence from colonial rule, weak governance has also plagued Africa and contributed significantly to the widespread poverty of its peoples. Only Botswana and offshore Mauritius have been governed democratically without interruption since independence. Both are among Africa's wealthiest countries, too, thanks to the steady application of good governance.

Aside from those two nations, and South Africa, Africa has been a continent of coups since 1960, with massive and oil-rich Nigeria suffering incessant periods of harsh, corrupt, autocratic military rule. Nearly every other country on or around the continent, small and large, has been plagued by similar bouts of instability and dictatorial rule. In the 1970s and 1980s Idi Amin ruled Uganda capriciously and Jean-Bedel Bokassa proclaimed himself emperor of the Central African Republic. Macias Nguema of Equatorial Guinea was another in that same mold. More recently Daniel arap Moi held Kenya in thrall and Robert Mugabe has imposed himself on once-prosperous Zimbabwe. In both of those cases, as in the case of Gnassingbe Eyadema in Togo and the late Mobutu Sese Seko in Congo, these presidents stole wildly and drove entire peoples and their nations into penury. Corruption is common in Africa, and so are a weak rule-of-law framework, misplaced development, high expenditures on soldiers and low expenditures on health and education, and a widespread (but not universal) refusal on the part of leaders to work well for their followers and citizens.

Conflict between groups within countries has also been common in Africa. More than 12 million Africans have been killed in civil wars since 1990, while another 9 million have become refugees. Decades of conflict in Sudan led to a January 2011 referendum in which the people of southern Sudan voted overwhelmingly to secede and form a new state. In early 2011, anti-government protests spread throughout North Africa, ultimately toppling long-standing regimes in Tunisia and Egypt. That same year, there were serious ongoing hostilities within Chad, Ivory Coast, Libya, the Niger Delta region of Nigeria, and Somalia.

Despite such dangers, despotism, and decay, Africa is improving. Botswana and Mauritius, now joined by South Africa, Senegal, Kenya, and Ghana, are beacons of democratic growth and enlightened rule. Uganda and Senegal are taking the lead in combating and reducing the spread of AIDS, and others are following. There are serious signs of the kinds of progressive economic policy changes that might lead to prosperity for more of Africa's peoples. The trajectory in Africa is positive.

Africa covers approximately one-fifth of the earth's land surface. The continent includes a variety of terrain and diverse plant and animal life. (Opposite) Spectacular Victoria Falls in Zimbabwe. (Right) A pair of zebras play together in the savanna of a nature reserve in Tanzania.

The Land

AFRICA IS THE SECOND largest of the world's seven continents, covering an area of nearly 11,700,000 square miles (around 30,300,000 square kilometers), or about 20 percent of the earth's land surface. It stretches for almost 5,000 miles (approximately 8,000 km) from its northern tip at Ras ben Sakka, Tunisia, to its most southerly point at Cape Agulhas, South Africa. At its widest point, it stretches 4,600 miles (7,400 km) from Cape Vert, Senegal, in the west to Ras Hafun, Somalia, in the east.

Africa is separated from Europe by the Mediterranean Sea. At the sea's narrowest point—in the Strait of Gibraltar—the two continents are only 15 miles (24 km) apart. The *Isthmus* of Suez separates Africa from Asia at Africa's far northeastern corner, and the continent has long coastlines with the Atlantic Ocean to the west and the Indian Ocean to the east.

GEOGRAPHY

Africa is one of the most geographically diverse of all the continents. It contains everything from snowcapped mountain peaks to grassy plains (known as *savannas*), dense rain forests, vast deserts, and long, stretching rivers.

The northern quarter of Africa is covered almost entirely by the vast Sahara, the largest desert in the world, spanning 3,500,000 square miles (9,065,000 sq km). It is sandy, hot, desolate, and, with the exception of a few *nomadic* tribes, virtually uninhabited. A narrow strip of fertile and irrigated land separates the Sahara from the Mediterranean coast. Most of the people of Morocco, Algeria, Tunisia, and Libya live along this fertile strip. Egypt is almost entirely desert; the only thing that makes the country inhabitable is the Nile River, which provides irrigation for farmland.

Bordering the Sahara, and separating it from the savanna farther to the south, is a strip of land known as the Sahel. Because of climate change and overuse by the tribes of herders who live in the Sahel, it is gradually receding and being replaced by desert. This process, known as desertification, has also become a problem in other regions of Africa.

Two other deserts cover much of southern Africa. The Kalahari, a barren area of reddish-brown sand, covers about 195,000 square miles (500,000 sq km). The Kalahari occupies most of the nation of Botswana as well as sections of Namibia and South Africa. In the local language of the area, *Kalahari* means "the great thirst," referring to its dry and unwelcoming environment. The Namib Desert is a narrow strip of desert running along the southwest coast of Africa, mostly in the country of Namibia. It covers roughly 13,000 square miles

The desolate Sahara is the largest desert in the world.

(34,000 sq km). The Namib has been described as "an ocean of sand," and it has the highest sand dunes in the world—some rise over 1,280 feet (390 meters).

Africa has several major mountain chains. In the northwest corner are the Atlas Mountains, running west to east and separating the Sahara from the coastal areas of Morocco, Algeria, and Tunisia. The highest peaks in the Atlas range rise over 8,000 feet (2,400 meters) and frequently are covered with snow in the winter. These mountains contain many fertile valleys that are home to millions of people.

Eastern Africa is very mountainous. The tallest peak in Africa, the volcanic Mount Kilimanjaro in Tanzania, soars 19,321 feet (5,889 meters). Mount Kenya, located just across the border from Kilimanjaro in neighboring

A view of Mount Kilimanjaro, the highest point in Africa.

Kenya, rises 17,057 feet (5,199 meters). Both Kilimanjaro and Kenya are permanently snowcapped.

Farther north, the mountainous country of Ethiopia contains several peaks with heights of 15,000 to 16,000 feet (4,500 to 4,900 meters). Another chain of mountains is located in West Africa, inland from the Gulf of Guinea. The highest peaks in this range, at over 13,000 feet (4,000 meters), are located in Cameroon.

Much of central Africa—often known as Equatorial Africa because of its proximity to the Equator—is tropical rain forest. The rain forest is hot and extremely humid, with heavy rainfall. It also is home to a vast range of animal and plant life. Bordering the rain forest to the north and south are savannas, an area characterized by tall grasses, scraggly bushes, and few trees. The savanna is home to the animals that Africa is most famous for—elephants, giraffes, gazelles, and zebras—as well as predator lions, cheetahs, and leopards.

One of the most interesting geographical features of East Africa is the Great Rift Valley, a deep rift, or split, in the earth that stretches from Syria in the Middle East to Mozambique. In places the valley has sheer walls over 1,000 feet (300 meters) deep. Africa's major lakes have formed along the Great Rift Valley. Lake Victoria, located on the border of Kenya, Tanzania, and Uganda, is the second-largest freshwater lake in the world (only Lake Superior is bigger). It also is the source of the world's longest river, the Nile, which flows north for 4,180 miles (6,688 km), and drains into the Mediterranean Sea in Egypt.

Other important rivers in Africa include the Niger, in West Africa, and the Congo, in central Africa. The Zambezi, also in central Africa, flows through six countries before emptying into the Indian Ocean. Along the way, the Zambezi thunders over Victoria Falls, a mile-wide sheet of water plunging 400 feet (120 meters), located along the border of Zimbabwe and Zambia.

The island of Madagascar, located in the Indian Ocean off the east coast of Africa, is the fourth-largest island in the world. It has a narrow coastal plain with a high plateau and mountains in the center. Its tallest peak is almost 10,000 feet (2,876 meters) high.

CLIMATE

The climate throughout much of Africa is tropical, which means it is generally very hot—at least during the day—with rainfall occurring seasonally. With the exception of the snowcapped mountains and high regions in South

Africa, the continent virtually never experiences freezing temperatures. Africa's deserts are extremely hot and dry; it is common for daytime temperatures to be over 100°F (40°C). At night, however, temperatures in the deserts can drop to 40°F (4°C).

In the rain forests, the temperature and humidity are high all year long, and heavy downpours occur all times of the year, often causing flooding. The seasons here are almost indistinguishable from one another. The coastal areas of West and East Africa that border the rain forests have a similar climate, except that heavy rainfall tends to occur only during certain times of year: north of the equator, the land receives heavy rainfall from April through September; and south of the equator, from October through March. The savannas also are hot, but receive much less rain than the rain forests, and usually only during the summer months.

The extreme north of Africa, along the Mediterranean coast, has the most moderate temperatures and the most recognizable seasons. Fall and winter are chilly and wet; summer is hot and humid; and spring is mild and pleasant. Extreme southern Africa has similar weather patterns, although it tends to be wetter and more humid than along the northern coast.

Madagascar's climate is tropical along the coast, arid in the south, and temperate in the mountainous central regions. Snowfall is frequent at the higher elevations, and the east coast faces drenching hurricanes and monsoons.

FLORA AND FAUNA

Africa is home to an extremely rich and diverse range of plant and animal life. Orange and olive trees thrive in the north, along the Mediterranean coast, and are important to the economies of Morocco, Algeria, and Tunisia. Oak, pine, myrtles, and cork trees also grow along the Mediterranean. The only significant plant that grows in the Sahara is the date palm, which grows in groves near *oases*. The African savanna is mostly coarse grassland, with a scattering of shrubs and trees. These low plants provide food for animals that live in the savanna. The most famous species of the savanna is the baobab, a hardy tree with a very thick trunk and spindly branches that is featured in many African stories and folk tales.

The most varied plant life is found in the dense and humid African rain forest, which covers much of the central part of the continent. In some areas the rain forest may contain over 3,000 species of trees and plants per square mile. The floor of the rain forest is covered with

Baobab trees like this one in Zambia are believed to live as long as 1,000 years. There is an African legend that explains why the tree's branches look like roots: a god disliked the tree and threw it out of his heavenly garden, but although it landed on Earth upside-down, it continued to grow.

ferns, shrubs, and other plants that require little sunlight (the dense forest prevents sunlight from reaching the floor). The next layer—up to an elevation of about 50 feet (17 meters)—contains woody trees and long vines. The highest section of the rain forest, known as the canopy, features tall evergreen trees with huge leaves.

Along the west and east coasts of Africa, the forest is less dense but the hot and humid weather still allows for a wide diversity of plant life. Many of the trees along the coastal regions have great agricultural value, and are cultivated for their fruits or nuts. In West Africa, coffee, cocoa, pineapple, and palm trees abound. In East Africa, cashew, coconut palm, and mango trees are common. Mangrove trees thrive along lagoons and tidal *estuaries*.

Madagascar has a unique *ecosystem*, distinguished from the rest of Africa or any other place in the world. Thousands of plant and animal

Ostriches are among the thousands of species of birds that can be found in Africa.

species on Madagascar are only found on the island, making it a favorite destination of biologists and botanists.

The species of the African savanna include some of the giants of the animal kingdom, such as elephants, rhinoceros, and giraffes—as well as some of the world's fiercest animals, such as lions, leopards, and hyenas. Zebras and graceful gazelles also inhabit the savanna, as does the cheetah, the fastest animal on earth.

Africa's forests are home to chimpanzees, gorillas, and baboons, and dozens of species of snakes—some of which are extremely poisonous. The rivers and streams of Africa's tropical regions serve as the habitat for hippopotamuses and crocodiles. The hot and humid climate of Africa's rain forests makes for an insect paradise. There are thousands of insect species in Africa, including scorpions, termites, and ants. One of the great *scourges* of Africa is the mosquito, which among other illnesses spreads malaria, a frequently fatal tropical disease. The bite of the tsetse fly, an insect that is endemic to Africa, can be fatal to cattle and cause debilitating sleeping sickness in humans.

Poachers have killed many of Africa's most majestic animals, such as elephants and gorillas. In addition, growing human populations have led to the destruction of natural habitats. To protect the most endangered species, a number of African countries have established game parks, which also serve as popular tourist attractions. Kenya, Tanzania, Cameroon, Zimbabwe, and South Africa, among others, have extensive game park systems.

QUICK FACTS: THE GEOGRAPHY OF AFRICA

Location: Divided by the equator, roughly half of Africa is in the Northern Hemisphere and half in the Southern Hemisphere. Africa is bounded on the north by the Mediterranean Sea, on the west by the Atlantic Ocean, and on the south and east by the Indian Ocean. Africa is completely surrounded by water except for a small border with Asia in the Sinai Peninsula.

Total area: 11,677,240 square miles (30,244,050 square kilometers)

Algeria: 952,696 sq miles (2,381,740 sq km)

Angola: 498,680 sq miles (1,246,700 sq km)

Benin: 45,048 sq miles (112,620 sq km)

Botswana: 240,148 sq miles (600,370 sq km)

Burkina Faso: 109,680 sq miles (274,200 sq km)

Burundi: 11,132 sq miles (27,830 sq km)

Cameroon: 190,176 sq miles (475,440 sq km)

Cape Verde: 1,559 sq miles (4,033 sq km)

Central African Republic: 249,193 sq miles (622,984 sq km)

Chad: 513,600 sq miles (1,284,000 sq km)

Comoros: 868 sq miles (2,170 sq km)

Democratic Republic of the Congo: 938,164 sq miles (2,345,410 sq km)

Republic of the Congo: 136,800 sq miles (342,000 sq km)

Djibouti: 9,200 sq miles (23,000 sq km)

Egypt: 400,580 sq miles (1,001,450 sq km)

Equatorial Guinea: 11,220 sq miles (28,051 sq km)

Eritrea: 48,528 sq miles (121,320 sq km)

Ethiopia: 450,850 sq miles (1,127,127 sq km)

Gabon: 107,066 sq miles (267,667 sq km)

The Gambia: 4,520 sq miles (11,300 sq km)

Ghana: 95,784 sq miles (239,460 sq km)

Guinea: 98,342 sq miles (245,857 sq km)

Guinea-Bissau: 14,448 sq miles (36,120 sq km)

Ivory Coast: 128,984 sq miles (322,460 sq km)

Kenya: 233,060 sq miles (582,650 sq km)

Lesotho: 12,142 sq miles (30,355 sq km)

Liberia: 44,548 sq miles (111,370 sq km)

Libya: 703,816 sq miles (1,759,540 sq km)

Madagascar: 231,816 sq miles (587,040 sq km)

Malawi: 47,392 sq miles (118,480 sq km)

Mali: 496,000 sq miles (1,240,000 sq km)

Mauritania: 412,280 sq miles (1,030,700 sq km)

Mauritius: 816 sq miles (2,040 sq km)

Morocco: 178,620 sq miles (446,550 sq km)

Mozambique: 320,636 sq miles (801,590 sq km)

Namibia: 330,167 sq miles (825,418 sq km)

Niger: 506,800 sq miles (1,267,000 sq km)

Nigeria: 369,507 sq miles (923,768 sq km)

Rwanda: 10,535 sq miles (26,338 sq km)

São Tomé and Príncipe: 400 sq miles (1,001 sq km)

Senegal: 78,476 sq miles (196,190 sq km)

Seychelles: 182 sq miles (455 sq km)

Sierra Leone: 28,696 sq miles (71,740 sq km)
Somalia: 255,062 sq miles (637,657 sq km)
South Africa: 487,964 sq miles (1,219,912 sq km)
South Sudan: 248,777 sq miles (644,329 sq km)
Sudan: 718,723 sq miles (1,861,484 sq km)
Swaziland: 6,945 sq miles (17,363 sq km)
Tanzania: 378,034 sq miles (945,087 sq km)
Togo: 22,714 sq miles (56,785 sq km)
Tunisia: 65,444 sq miles (163,610 sq km)
Uganda: 94,416 sq miles (236,040 sq km)
Western Sahara (claimed by Morocco): 106,400 sq miles (266,000 sq km)
Zambia: 301,045 sq miles (752,614 sq km)
Zimbabwe: 156,232 sq miles (390,580 sq km)

Terrain: The north is largely covered by the vast Sahara Desert, with the exception of an arable strip of land bordering the Mediterranean coast. The central part of the continent is mostly dense rain forest, surrounded by grassy savanna and separated from the desert by a semi-arid region known as the Sahel. Great mountains dominate the eastern part of the continent, and lesser mountain chains can be found in the west and northwest. There are two smaller deserts in the south.

Climate: Tropical in much of central Africa, with hot temperatures and periods of heavy rain. Desert regions are hot and dry. The Mediterranean coast is temperate, as are coastal regions in the far south and east. Mountainous regions can be quite cold, with sub-freezing temperatures and snowfall.

Natural resources: Oil and gas, gold, diamonds, iron ore, bauxite, phosphorous, fisheries, fertile soils

Elevation extremes:
Lowest point: Lac Assal (Lake Assal) in Djibouti, 502 feet (153 meters) below sea level
Highest point: Mount Kilimanjaro in Tanzania, 19,321 feet (5,889 meters)

Natural hazards: Drought, heavy rains and flooding, earthquakes

Source: CIA World Factbook, 2012.

Africa is known as the "cradle of civilization." (Opposite) The Sphinx and Great Pyramid at Giza are among the most recognized remains of ancient Egypt, one of the world's earliest civilizations. (Right) The work of Dr. Louis Leakey in Tanzania's Olduvai Gorge during the 1950s and 1960s contributed a great deal to the understanding of human origins.

2 The History

MANY RESEARCHERS AND scientists believe that humans first appeared in Africa about 200,000 years ago. *Archaeologists* and *anthropologists* have found fossils and other evidence of human life in the Great Rift Valley of East Africa and in the Afar region of Ethiopia. These discoveries have led to the conclusion that Africa was indeed the "cradle of human civilization." Experts surmise that about 100,000 years ago, some of these early humans migrated out of Africa and very gradually spread throughout the planet. If this theory is true, then *all* human beings have African roots.

The early humans who remained in Africa were primarily hunters and gatherers, living in small communities along riverbanks or near lakes and constantly moving in search of food. Because of the abundance of wildlife and the warm climate, food was generally easy to find, except during periods of drought. Around 10,000 years ago, the early Africans began to raise animals—such as goats and sheep—and plant crops. With the development of methods of farming, the population grew larger and became settled in permanent villages and communities.

EARLY AFRICAN CIVILIZATIONS

Large numbers of early Africans migrated north out of the Rift Valley to the fertile land along the Nile River in northeast Africa. These communities eventually formed two empires, known today as Upper Egypt and Lower Egypt. By around 3000 B.C., these empires had merged into one great kingdom, thereby launching one of the greatest civilizations in history.

The rulers of Egypt were hereditary kings known as pharaohs, who were believed to be divine figures. The Egyptians developed an elaborate and complex belief system that emphasized honoring powerful gods and preparing for the afterlife. Some of the great temples and monuments they built still stand today. The most impressive of these are the Great Pyramids, which served as tombs for powerful pharaohs. They are among the world's architectural and engineering wonders.

Egyptians also invented paper (made from a fibrous plant called *papyrus*); made advances in astronomy, medicine, and other fields; and developed one of the world's first written languages. Egypt was ruled by a succession of pharaohs until 332 B.C., when the armies of the Macedonian conqueror Alexander the Great occupied Egypt. This ushered in a long era of invasions and foreign rule that did not come to a complete end until 1952.

Several powerful African empires rose up in West Africa beginning around A.D. 400. The empire of Ghana developed an elaborate trading system with peoples in North Africa and, beginning around 800, with Arabs to the east and north. Ghana's wealth was founded on its vast gold mines. Merchants traded gold for salt and other goods, and artisans created beautiful gold jewelry. Little is known about how the empire of Ghana was ruled or what life was like, but at its height it undoubtedly was a very powerful and wealthy kingdom.

Around 1200 a new West African power, the empire of Mali, rose to prominence and surpassed Ghana in both wealth and influence. At the height of its power in the mid-14th century, Mali controlled trade in gold and salt throughout much of west and northwest Africa. Two cities of the empire became centers of trade and Islamic learning—Djenne, and later, the legendary Timbuktu. But by the late 15th century, these cities and other parts of Mali had been conquered by the empire of Songhai, at that time led by the great Sonni Ali. In existence for eight centuries, and at one point the largest empire in West Africa, Songhai was based in what is now central Nigeria and once stretched as far north as Niger and Mali and as far west as Senegal. Sonni Ali and his successor, Askia Muhammad, were the empire's greatest rulers and had the most success spreading Islam throughout the region.

Other West African powers that gradually became more powerful during Mali's decline were the Hausa states and the Ashanti Kingdom. The Ashanti, who were based in what is now Ghana, became famous for their craftsmanship in gold, ivory, textiles, and iron. They also developed a formidable military that dominated neighboring peoples at the height of their power in the 17th century. Around this time, the Ashanti participated in the slave trade by selling other Africans—usually men they had captured in battle—to European slave traders. Many of these slaves ended up in European colonies in North and South America.

The most powerful kingdom that rose to power in central Africa was the Kongo. It emerged around 1400, along the southwest coast of Africa. The Kongo grew into one of Africa's largest empires, based on the trade of copper, iron, and—beginning in the 16th century—slaves. Most of the slaves sold by the Kongo were bought by Portuguese slave traders, who then shipped them to the Portuguese colony in Brazil.

The first great power to ascend in southern Africa was the Great Zimbabwe, whose wealth derived from cattle herding and the gold trade. It lasted from around 1200 to around 1500. The only power that rivaled the Great Zimbabwe in influence was the Zulu tribe, which rose to prominence in the early 1800s. Its greatest warrior-leader was Emperor Shaka, who ruled from 1816 to 1828. He attacked and plundered neighboring peoples as he greatly expanded the Zulu realm. An offshoot group of the Zulu conquered the Great Zimbabwe, but failed to establish a unified state as rulers had done in previous eras.

In East Africa, the dominant people were a loosely united group known as the Swahili, who lived along the coast from modern-day Mozambique to modern-day Somalia. They all spoke the same language (also called Swahili), and established thriving trade relationships with Arabia and India, selling ivory, gold, and slaves. The Swahili lived in dozens of port cities spread along the East African coast, including Mogadishu, today the capital of

Somalia; Mombasa, in modern-day Kenya; and Zanzibar, an island that is now part of Tanzania.

FOREIGN INVASIONS AND COLONIZATION

Because of its proximity to Europe, North Africa was subject to invasion from the time of the earliest civilizations. Phoenicians, Greeks, Romans, and others explored, conquered, and settled parts of North Africa as early as the ninth century B.C. For hundreds of years, the coastal city of Carthage was the main trading center of the Mediterranean world until it became engaged in a series of wars against Rome, at that time a rising European city-state. Rome ultimately prevailed in the Punic Wars, and Carthage was destroyed in 146 B.C.

By A.D. 120, the Roman Empire had secure control of the entire African coast between Morocco and Egypt. (The word *Africa* in fact comes from Latin, the language of the Roman Empire. It first was used in reference to what today is Tunisia, and was later applied to the entire continent.) North Africa remained under the control of the Roman Empire until the fifth century, when Germanic tribes invaded from Europe and sacked Roman cities. However, even after the fall of Rome around A.D. 476, North Africa remained under the control of the powerful Byzantine Empire, the eastern half of the Roman Empire.

By 646, the Byzantines were faced with a new danger from the east. Arab armies spreading the new Islamic religion invaded North Africa and quickly gained control over the entire area. In a few centuries, Islam was the dominant religion of North Africa, and through trade and other contacts the religion spread across the Sahara deep into West Africa. Beginning in the eighth

A group of Muslims meet outside of a mosque in Asmara, Eritrea. Conquering Arab armies spread Islam into North Africa in the seventh century, and the religion spread across East Africa through trade and missionary work. Today, Islam and Christianity are the predominant religions in Africa.

century, Muslims moved south down the east coast of Africa, converting the Swahilis and expanding the already vibrant trade with the Arabian Peninsula.

In many places Islam supplanted the religion common throughout the Roman Empire—Christianity. Christians had been preaching in North Africa as early as A.D. 100, long before the empire accepted Christianity as a legitimate religion, around A.D. 313. The Aksum Empire, located in the region that is now northern Ethiopia, converted to Christianity in the 4th century. Although the religion did not spread as widely as Islam, by the time of the first Arab invasion there were sizable Christian communities throughout North Africa, especially in Egypt and Ethiopia. The people of these communities resisted the pressures to convert to Islam, and to this day there are significant Christian minorities in Egypt and Ethiopia. With the advent of European colonialism, missionaries gained entry into Africa and spread Christianity to many of the non-Muslim areas.

Sailors and adventurers from Portugal began to explore the coast of Africa in the 15th century. Over a period of about 80 years, the Portuguese sent expeditions south. These surveyors mapped sections of the coast not known to Europe, and initially disregarded the interior, limiting their activities to trading for gold, ivory, and slaves. In 1497–99 Vasco da Gama made a historic voyage around the huge continent, landing at ports in East Africa and then in India. This opened a trade route with the east that would make tiny Portugal very wealthy.

During the early 1800s, European explorers, fascinated by Africa's many mysteries, began to undertake journeys into the interior. The most famous of

In the 15th century the Portuguese began to chart the coast of Africa and to trade with the people of the continent; the flags on this map from 1501, a few years after the return of Vasco da Gama, show the locations of Portuguese trading posts. Over the next five centuries Europeans would involve themselves heavily in African affairs and establish control over much of the continent.

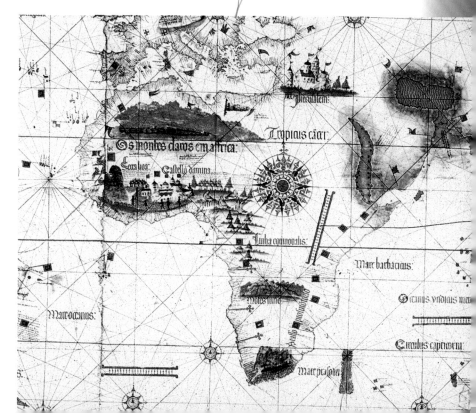

them, the Scotsman David Livingstone, became the first European to cross Africa from east to west.

Later in the 19th century, the rivalries between the major European states extended to competition for territories in Africa. One after another, the European powers seized and claimed parts of the continent. The African peoples often put up fierce resistance to colonization, but were no match for the modern weaponry of the Europeans. The French focused on North and West Africa; the British on southern and eastern Africa and Egypt; and the Portuguese on the southwestern and southeastern coasts. In addition, the Belgians established a foothold in what is today the Democratic Republic of the Congo; Dutch settlers moved into southern Africa; and the Germans claimed territory in East Africa. In order to avoid confrontation and prevent conflict, the European powers met in Berlin during 1884–85 to formally divide Africa among themselves. In creating artificial boundaries throughout Africa, the Berlin Conference gave no consideration to the needs or desires of the African people.

While the 1884–85 conference prevented a war over territorial claims in Africa, the major European war that broke out in 1914 still entangled the African people in conflict. Over 2 million Africans were forced to fight for their respective European colonial masters during World War I, and tens of thousands were killed.

After the war, increasing numbers of Africans started to demand an end to colonialism. Political organizations formed in many parts of Africa, with the goal of achieving independence. The colonial powers tried to suppress these organizations and their leaders, but the movements continued to grow throughout the 1920s and 1930s. In 1922, Britain reluctantly granted independence to Egypt, though the British still maintained significant control over Egyptian politics and the economy.

Only two other African countries were fully independent: Liberia, which had been founded by freed American slaves in 1847; and Ethiopia, the only African country that had not fallen under colonial rule. But in 1935, Italy—then an ally of Nazi Germany—invaded and occupied Ethiopia. By 1941, however, African forces had driven the Italians out, a victory that gave a tremendous boost to advocates of African independence in other countries. Although Africans wanted independence, most supported the British and French efforts against Germany and its allies during World War II. Many African soldiers fought bravely on the side of the allies against Germany in North Africa, and against Japanese forces in Burma. Thousands of African troops took part in the allied invasion of Italy in 1943. After the war ended in 1945, however, Egypt, Liberia, and Ethiopia remained the only independent countries in Africa.

INDEPENDENCE

The world changed dramatically after the end of the Second World War. The two largest colonial powers, Great Britain and France, realized that they could no longer afford to maintain their vast colonial empires. India's success in achieving independence from Great Britain in 1947 was an inspiration to all colonized nations.

Moreover, a new generation of *charismatic* African leaders had emerged. Many were well educated and skilled at political organization. Among the most

Kwame Nkrumah of Ghana addresses the United Nations, 1961. Under Nkrumah's leadership, in 1957 Ghana became the first country of sub-saharan African to gain independence from colonial rule.

famous and influential independence leaders were Leopold Senghor of Senegal, Félix Houphouët-Boigny of the Ivory Coast (also known as Côte d'Ivoire), Kwame Nkrumah of Ghana, and Julius Nyerere of Tanzania. One by one, starting in the late 1950s, African countries began winning their independence. By 1960, nearly all of France's African colonies had been declared independent. With the exception of Algeria, which won its independence after a long and brutal civil war in 1962, these colonies were freed without bloodshed. Most of Britain's colonies had achieved independence by 1965. By 1970, there were 43 independent countries in Africa.

There were a few exceptions to the great African independence movement of the 1950s and 1960s. Portugal held onto its African colonies of Angola and Mozambique, despite long and bloody rebellions in both countries, until 1975. The other exceptions were South Africa and Zimbabwe (South Africa was not a colony after 1910, though technically it remained a part of the British Commonwealth.) Sizable white minorities controlled the government and the economic system in each country. Both countries established a racist social and political system under which the black majority was suppressed and dominated (South Africa's system was known as *apartheid*). Zimbabwe finally achieved majority rule in 1980, but South Africa did not become a truly free country until black majority rule was established in 1994, following decades of often-violent struggle.

GROWING PAINS

The newly independent African countries faced daunting problems. When the European powers divided up Africa after the Berlin Conference, they paid little attention to where various ethnic groups lived. Thus, most African countries were home to several different peoples, often those who historically had been rivals or enemies. People were often more loyal to their ethnic group, religion, or local clan than they were to the new country that they were now citizens of. This has led to border disputes, violence, and even civil war. Between 1967 and 1970, Nigeria was devastated by a civil war that left over one million people dead. Other civil wars raged in Angola, the Democratic Republic of the Congo (formerly Zaire), Ethiopia, Somalia, Sudan, Chad, Liberia, Rwanda, Burundi, and Sierra Leone (as of this writing, war or civil strife still rages in Liberia, Sierra Leone, and Sudan). These conflicts made millions of Africans refugees, often dependent upon charitable organizations for their very survival.

Nelson Mandela votes in South Africa's historic 1994 election that marked the end of apartheid rule in South Africa.

Most African countries also had a difficult time establishing stable political systems, in part because of ethnic tensions, and in part because the colonial powers had generally made no effort to create political institutions. Many states suffered from military *coups*, or from *authoritarian* leaders who ruled ruthlessly. In addition, Africa's independence coincided with the start of the *cold war* between the United States and the Soviet Union, which meant that both superpowers actively sought allies and military bases in Africa's newly independent countries. Frequently, the United States and the Soviet Union helped to keep ruthless dictators in power simply because they promised to offer support in the cold war struggle. Few African countries were democracies, and most were one-party states.

Virtually all the countries of the continent suffered from economic hardship. The European colonial rulers had seen Africa as a source of commodities and raw materials, and thus did not see the need to help colonies develop diversified economic systems. Dependence on commodities—such as agricultural products and minerals—meant that African countries suffered if the international demand for these commodities fell. Conditions beyond a government's control, such as drought, could quickly lead to widespread famine and economic collapse. The lack of good educational and health care systems also hindered economic growth.

African countries borrowed billions of dollars from the governments and banks of Europe and the United States in order to pay for economic development projects such as roads, schools, power plants, factories, and airports. Many of these projects turned out to be unproductive or badly managed, leaving the countries even poorer and in great debt.

AFRICA TODAY

As the 21st century begins, Africa continues to face serious problems. It remains the world's poorest continent, producing less than 5 percent of the world's *gross domestic product (GDP)* even though it was home to about 15 percent of the world's population by 2012. Seventy percent of the world's poorest countries are in Africa.

The continent's great poverty has many consequences, including inadequate health care. Life expectancy in the 20 poorest African countries is less than 51 years, and many children die in infancy. Diseases such as HIV/AIDS, tuberculosis, and malaria are widespread, and public health care systems are crumbling under the pressure. AIDS is the leading cause of death in sub-Saharan Africa, with an estimated 22.5 million people infected with the HIV/AIDS virus by 2010. Most Africans have no access to good hospitals or the latest medicines.

Poverty has impeded Africans in many countries from even getting a modest education. Low levels of educational achievement only lead to greater poverty and despair for most countries. Moreover, Africa's rapidly growing population creates new stresses on both the health care and educational systems.

Africa's political systems have been largely unable to address the continent's serious problems. After the cold war came to an end, the leading powers had less interest in propping up the governments of friendly African dictators and instead began urging African countries to establish democracies, with elections and multiple political parties. A number of states started to

Salva Kiir Mayardit (center), president of the newly formed Republic of South Sudan, prepares to declare independence at a public ceremony, July 2011. Sudan was divided into two countries as a result of a 2005 peace agreement that ended more than two decades of conflict between the Arab Muslim majority of northern Sudan and the black Christians who lived in the south.

move toward this kind of democracy, but the process often was undermined by ethnic rivalries and conflicts that, once suppressed by the dictators, now rose to the surface. Today, only a handful of African countries are true democracies, though more and more Africans are demanding that their governments be democratic and grant them civil freedoms.

During 2010 and 2011, widespread protests in North African countries led to the removement of several longtime leaders from power, including Hosni Mubarak of Egypt and Zine El Abidine Ben Ali of Tunisia. In Libya, a civil war broke out that resulted in the ouster of dictator Muammar Gaddafi. In October 2011, rebel forces captured and killed Gaddafi.

However, even if more of Africa's countries were to institute legitimate democratic forms of government, there is no guarantee that they could peacefully resolve ethnic and religious disputes. During the first decade of the 21st century, ethnic and religious conflicts occurred in Sudan, Ivory Coast, Rwanda, Burundi, Nigeria, and the Democratic Republic of the Congo. In too many cases, these have reached the level of *genocide*. Other African countries face tensions that could potentially explode into violence at any time.

All of these problems—poverty, poor education and health care, unstable political systems, and ethnic or religious violence—contribute to Africa's ongoing economic crisis. Based on its abundance of natural resources and human capital, Africa should be among the wealthiest continents in the world. The challenge for African governments and people in the 21st century is to achieve their true economic potential. To do so will require stable governments, open economies, foreign investment, and a real commitment to improving educational opportunities.

The new Libyan flag flies as a man watches from the balcony of his bullet-riddled home in Zawiya, a center of the rebellion against longtime Libyan dictator Muammar Gaddafi.

(Opposite) A hippopotamus gapes in one of central Africa's rivers. Tourism, which is largely based on wildlife, is an economic mainstay of several African countries. (Right) At 1,969 feet (600 m) high and 1,903 feet (580 m) long, the Kariba Dam is one of the largest in the world. The hydroelectric dam provides power to Zambia and Zimbabwe.

3 The Economy

ALTHOUGH AFRICA IS THE poorest continent, the picture is not totally bleak. Its countries possess vast natural resources, rich and fertile soils, and a young and *entrepreneurial* work force.

Even in the midst of Africa's economic problems, a few countries—such as South Africa, Botswana, Tunisia, and the small island nation of Mauritius—have managed to create very successful economies with standards of living approaching that of the developed world. Other African countries, such as the oil-rich nations of Algeria, Angola, and Nigeria, have great potential to succeed economically. Many specialists on Africa believe that the continent's economic problems need not be permanent; to them, it is a question of adopting the correct economic policies.

Upon achieving independence, the majority of African countries put into place *socialist* systems in which the central government attempted to manage the entire economy. These policies almost always failed. Even worse, corrupt authoritarian leaders frequently stole their country's wealth for their personal use. The large export sums that were generated from the continent's natural resources rarely found its way to the average African, who struggled for daily survival.

During the 1980s and 1990s, African nations found themselves under intense pressure to reform their economies and establish *free markets*. The pressure came not only from their citizens, but also from international organizations such as the World Bank and the International Monetary Fund (IMF). For several decades, these organizations had loaned or donated billions of dollars to African countries for economic development projects to improve the lives of African citizens, but had seen very little success. They started to demand that African nations reform their economies and put an end to corruption and mismanagement. Continued assistance was made conditional on these reforms.

Africa's economic development has become a hotly debated issue. Growing numbers of Africans and their sympathizers in the developed world have become critical of the reforms demanded by the World Bank, IMF, and other foreign lending organizations. They claim that these reforms have only led to the enrichment of a few people, while the majority of Africans remain mired in hopeless poverty. On the other side of the debate are specialists who say the reforms African states have implemented have not gone far enough, and that the answer is an even more radical transformation of economic policy. The only thing both sides agree on is that, a few positive cases notwithstanding, Africa is in a state of economic stagnation.

AGRICULTURE

Subsistence agriculture is the way of life for a majority of Africans. In other words, they grow the food they and their families need to survive, and trade the excess when it is available in a local market for non-agricultural necessities. When growing conditions are good, subsistence farmers can survive and sometimes live comfortably. But drought or floods can quickly lead to disaster, including famine and starvation.

Agricultural products are also major export items for many African countries. Africa produces much of the world's coffee, cocoa, pineapples, coconuts, and palm oil. Cotton is a principal source of export income for Egypt, Sudan, Mali, and Benin. Tanzania, Mozambique, and Kenya export much of the world's cashew nuts, and Madagascar supplies much of the world's vanilla beans and cloves. North Africa is a major producer and exporter of olive oil, dates, and citrus fruits. Fresh-cut flowers are grown in countries such as Kenya and Ivory Coast and shipped overnight by plane to

Egyptians pick cotton in a field along the fertile banks of the Nile River.

flower markets in Europe. Because Africa's climate allows for year-round growth in many areas, fresh fruits and vegetables are exported during the European winter.

Fishing is an important source of livelihood along coastal areas and around the major lakes. Much of the catch is for local consumption, but some countries, such as Morocco and Mauritania in northwest Africa, have become important exporters of fish.

PETROLEUM AND MINERALS

Africa has extensive reserves of oil and natural gas and is a major exporter of both. The North African nation of Libya holds the world's fifth-largest reserves of oil, and the reserves of neighboring Algeria are the tenth largest in the world. Angola, Congo, Egypt, Gabon, and Nigeria are other significant producers of oil.

Africa is also a continent rich in mineral resources. One of the things that first attracted European explorers to Africa was its abundance of gold and diamonds. Twenty-five percent of the world's gold is mined in Africa, with over half of that amount coming from South Africa. Botswana, the Democratic Republic of the Congo (DRC), and South Africa are among the world's top six producers of diamonds. DeBeers, a huge South African company, leads the world in diamond production and marketing. New deposits of gold and diamonds are often uncovered, and mining companies are always searching for new opportunities. Unfortunately, several of the civil wars that have raged in Central and West Africa have been fueled in part by competition over diamonds and gold.

Among the other important minerals found in abundance in Africa are platinum (South Africa and Zimbabwe), copper (Zambia and DRC), cobalt (DRC, Zambia, and Zimbabwe), zinc (DRC), bauxite (Guinea), uranium (South Africa and Chad), and phosphates (Morocco). Mauritania contains one of the world's largest deposits of iron ore.

Minerals and mining make up the largest export revenue for about a dozen African countries. Because the prices of gold, diamonds, and other minerals regularly fluctuate according to supply and demand, the revenues of these countries are in turn subject to dramatic swings.

INDUSTRY

Africa is the least industrialized continent in the world. However, industry does play an important role in several of Africa's larger countries, and virtually every country has some small-scale industry and manufacturing. Both South Africa and Egypt produce automobiles and other vehicles, and a number of countries have factories that produce vehicle parts and supplies. Algeria, Egypt, Morocco, and Tunisia manufacture chemical and *petrochemical* products, which they export to Europe, as well as *pharmaceuticals*. South Africa also is a major chemical-producing nation. Egypt and South Africa have large aluminum and steel plants, and several other African countries have smaller steel mills that produce steel for local use.

Food and beverage production is a growing industry in much of Africa. Some small factories in Africa's larger cities produce canned vegetables or fruit juices. Many countries produce a local beer and soft drinks (usually under license to international companies, such as Coca-Cola). South Africa,

Morocco, and Tunisia make wines that are exported to foreign markets. Other small-scale factories in African cities manufacture soap, furniture, or simple household goods.

Virtually every African country has a textile industry, which typically produces handmade traditional clothing for the local market. Only Egypt, Tunisia, and Mauritius produce large quantities of textiles and clothing for the world market. Morocco is one of the world's largest manufacturers of footwear.

Arts and crafts remain an important traditional industry in Africa's villages and small towns. Artisans make colorful textiles, carved wooden or stone masks, and jewelry for the local market as well as for tourists and exporters. While the arts and crafts industry is not a significant source of national income in most countries, it does provide a number of jobs and helps African societies hold onto their histories and traditions.

The global technology industry has largely bypassed Africa. The rate of Internet access is extremely low, and very few individuals own personal computers. The one exception is telecommunication. Wireless technology has spread rapidly across Africa, and has been a great benefit to outlying areas that were never connected to telephone lines.

TOURISM

One economic sector that many Africans hope to grow and expand is tourism. Africa contains beautiful beaches, rugged mountains, fascinating cities, tropical rain forests, and savannas filled with wildlife. Its warm climate offers relief from the cold winters of the Northern Hemisphere, and its musical and artistic traditions have attracted foreigners for centuries.

Egypt is already a prime tourist destination, and has been for decades. It earns substantial income from the millions of tourists who travel there every year to visit its ancient pyramids and temples or beach resorts of the Red Sea. Morocco, home to some of the most alluring cities in Arab North Africa, also attracts millions of tourists each year, many of whom are from nearby European nations. Kenya and Tanzania support sizable tourism industries that are founded on wildlife and mountain climbing. South Africa, a country with great natural diversity and modern cities, has become one of Africa's leading tourist destinations. The west coast of Africa has beautiful beaches and pleasant cities, and attracts thousands of Europeans in search of warm weather during the winter. Many African Americans in search of their heritage visit West African countries.

For Africa to develop its full potential as a tourist destination, the tourism infrastructure of many nations—hotels, restaurants, transportation systems, and travel agencies—still needs to be modernized and improved. Political instability and ethnic conflict also hinder tourism's expansion. Liberia, for example, has beautiful beaches and an English-speaking population, but years of civil war have destroyed much of the infrastructure and made it a dangerous place to visit.

The World Bank and other international aid agencies have made tourism development one of their priorities for Africa, and many African countries are determined to make tourism a growth industry for the 21st century.

QUICK FACTS: THE LEADING PRODUCTS OF AFRICAN NATIONS

Algeria
Agriculture: wheat, barley, oats, grapes, olives, citrus, fruits, sheep, cattle
Industry/mining: petroleum, natural gas, light industries, mining, electrical, petrochemical, food processing

Angola
Agriculture: bananas, sugarcane, coffee, sisal, corn, cotton, manioc (tapioca), tobacco, vegetables, plantains, livestock, forest products, fish
Industry/mining: petroleum, iron ore, diamonds, phosphates, gold, feldspar, bauxite, uranium, cement, basic metal products, fish processing, food processing, brewing, tobacco products, sugar, textiles

Benin
Agriculture: cotton, corn, cassava (tapioca), yams, beans, palm oil, peanuts, livestock
Industry/mining: textiles, food processing, chemical production, construction materials

Botswana
Agriculture: livestock, sorghum, maize, millet, beans, sunflowers, groundnuts
Industry/Mining: diamonds, copper, nickel, salt, soda ash, potash, livestock processing, textiles

Burkina Faso
Agriculture: cotton, peanuts, shea nuts, sesame, sorghum, millet, corn, rice, livestock

Industry/mining: cotton lint, beverages, agricultural processing, soap, cigarettes, textiles, gold

Burundi
Agriculture: coffee, cotton, tea, corn, sorghum, sweet potatoes, bananas, manioc, beef, milk, hides
Industry/mining: light consumer goods such as blankets, shoes, soap, assembly of imported components, public works construction, food processing

Cameroon
Agriculture: coffee, cocoa, cotton, rubber, bananas, oilseed, grains, root starches, livestock, timber
Industry/mining: petroleum production and refining, food processing, light consumer goods, textiles, lumber

Cape Verde
Agriculture: bananas, corn, beans, sweet potatoes, sugarcane, coffee, peanuts; fish
Industry/mining: food and beverages, fish processing, shoes and garments, salt mining, ship repair

Central African Republic
Agriculture: cotton, coffee, tobacco, manioc (tapioca), yams, millet, corn, bananas, timber
Industry/mining: diamond mining, logging, brewing, textiles, footwear, assembly of bicycles and motorcycles

Chad
Agriculture: cotton, sorghum, millet, peanuts, rice, potatoes,

manioc, cattle, sheep, goats, camels
Industry/mining: oil, cotton textiles, meatpacking, beer brewing, natron (sodium carbonate), soap, cigarettes, construction materials

Comoros
Agriculture: vanilla, cloves, perfume essences, copra, coconuts, bananas, cassava (tapioca)
Industry/mining: tourism, perfume distillation

Democratic Republic of the Congo
Agriculture: coffee, sugar, palm oil, rubber, tea, quinine, cassava (tapioca), palm oil, bananas, root crops, corn, fruits, wood products
Industry/mining: mining (diamonds, copper, zinc), mineral processing, consumer products (including textiles, footwear, cigarettes, processed foods and beverages), cement

Republic of the Congo
Agriculture: cassava (tapioca), sugar, rice, corn, peanuts, vegetables, coffee, cocoa, forest products
Industry/mining: petroleum extraction, cement, lumber, brewing, sugar, palm oil, soap, flour, cigarettes

Djibouti
Agriculture: fruits, vegetables, goats, sheep, camels
Industry/mining: construction, agricultural processing

Egypt

Agriculture: cotton, rice, corn, wheat, beans, fruits, vegetables, cattle, water buffalo, sheep, goats
Industry/mining: textiles, food processing, tourism, chemicals, hydrocarbons, construction, cement, metals

Equatorial Guinea

Agriculture: coffee, cocoa, rice, yams, cassava (tapioca), bananas, palm oil nuts, livestock, timber
Industry/mining: petroleum, fishing, sawmilling, natural gas

Eritrea

Agriculture: sorghum, lentils, vegetables, corn, cotton, tobacco, coffee, sisal, livestock, goats, fish
Industry/mining: food processing, beverages, clothing and textiles

Ethiopia

Agriculture: cereals, pulses, coffee, oilseed, sugarcane, potatoes, khat, hides, cattle, sheep, goats
Industry/mining: food processing, beverages, textiles, chemicals, metals processing, cement

Gabon

Agriculture: cocoa, coffee, sugar, palm oil, rubber, cattle, *okoume* (a tropical softwood), fish
Industry/mining: petroleum extraction and refining, manganese, and gold mining, chemicals, ship repair, food and beverage, textile, lumbering and plywood, cement

The Gambia

Agriculture: rice, millet, sorghum, peanuts, corn, sesame, cassava (tapioca), palm kernels, cattle, sheep, goats
Industry/mining: processing peanuts, fish, and hides, tourism, beverages, agricultural machinery assembly, woodworking, metalworking, clothing

Ghana

Agriculture: cocoa, rice, coffee, cassava (tapioca), peanuts, corn, shea nuts, bananas, timber
Industry/mining: mining, lumbering, light manufacturing, aluminum smelting, food processing

Guinea

Agriculture: rice, coffee, pineapples, palm kernels, cassava (tapioca), bananas, sweet potatoes, cattle, sheep, goats, timber
Industry/mining: bauxite, gold, diamonds, alumina refining, light manufacturing and agricultural processing industries

Guinea-Bissau

Agriculture: rice, corn, beans, fish, cassava, cashew nuts, peanuts, palm kernels, cotton, timber
Industry/mining: agricultural products processing, beer, soft drinks

Ivory Coast

Agriculture: coffee, cocoa beans, bananas, palm kernels, corn, rice, manioc (tapioca), sweet potatoes, sugar, cotton, rubber, timber

Industry/mining: foodstuffs, beverages, wood products, oil refining, truck and bus assembly, textiles, fertilizer, building materials, electricity

Kenya

Agriculture: tea, coffee, corn, wheat, sugarcane, fruit, vegetables, dairy products, beef, pork, poultry, eggs
Industry/mining: small-scale consumer goods (plastic, furniture, batteries, textiles, soap, cigarettes, flour), agricultural products processing, oil refining, cement, tourism

Lesotho

Agriculture: corn, wheat, pulses, sorghum, barley, livestock
Industry/mining: food, beverages, textiles, apparel assembly, handicrafts, construction, tourism

Liberia

Agriculture: rubber, coffee, cocoa, rice, cassava (tapioca), palm oil, sugarcane, bananas, sheep, goats, timber
Industry/mining: rubber processing, palm oil processing, timber, diamonds

Libya

Agriculture: wheat, barley, olives, dates, citrus, vegetables, peanuts, soybeans, cattle
Industry/mining: petroleum, food processing, textiles, handicrafts, cement

Source: CIA World Factbook, 2011

Madagascar

Agriculture: coffee, vanilla, sugarcane, cloves, cocoa, rice, cassava (tapioca), beans, bananas, peanuts, livestock products

Industry/mining: meat processing, soap, breweries, tanneries, sugar, textiles, glassware, cement, automobile assembly plant, paper, petroleum, tourism

Malawi

Agriculture: tobacco, sugarcane, cotton, tea, corn, potatoes, cassava (tapioca), sorghum, pulses, groundnuts, Macadamia nuts, cattle, goats

Industry/mining: tobacco, tea, sugar, sawmill products, cement, consumer goods

Mali

Agriculture: cotton, millet, rice, corn, vegetables, peanuts, cattle, sheep, goats

Industry/mining: food processing, construction, phosphate and gold mining

Mauritania

Agriculture: dates, millet, sorghum, rice, corn, dates, cattle, sheep

Industry/mining: fish processing, mining of iron ore and gypsum

Mauritius

Agriculture: sugarcane, tea, corn, potatoes, bananas, pulses, cattle, goats, fish

Industry/mining: food processing (largely sugar milling), textiles, clothing, chemicals, metal products, transport equipment, nonelectrical machinery, tourism

Morocco

Agriculture: barley, wheat, citrus, wine, vegetables, olives, livestock

Industry/mining: phosphate rock mining and processing, food processing, leather goods, textiles, construction, tourism

Mozambique

Agriculture: cotton, cashew nuts, sugarcane, tea, cassava (tapioca), corn, coconuts, sisal, citrus and tropical fruits, potatoes, sunflowers, beef, poultry

Industry/mining: food, beverages, chemicals (fertilizer, soap, paints), aluminum, petroleum products, textiles, cement, glass, asbestos, tobacco

Namibia

Agriculture: millet, sorghum, peanuts, livestock, fish

Industry/mining: meatpacking, fish processing, dairy products, mining (diamond, lead, zinc, tin, silver, tungsten, uranium, copper)

Niger

Agriculture: cowpeas, cotton, peanuts, millet, sorghum, cassava (tapioca), rice, cattle, sheep, goats, camels, donkeys, horses, poultry

Industry/mining: uranium mining, cement, brick, textiles, food processing, chemicals, slaughterhouses

Nigeria

Agriculture: cocoa, peanuts, palm oil, corn, rice, sorghum, millet, cassava (tapioca), yams, rubber, cattle, sheep, goats, pigs, timber, fish

Industry/mining: crude oil, coal, tin, columbite, palm oil, peanuts, cotton, rubber, wood, hides and skins, textiles, cement and other construction materials, food products, footwear, chemicals, fertilizer, printing, ceramics, steel

Rwanda

Agriculture: coffee, tea, pyrethrum (insecticide made from chrysanthemums), bananas, beans, sorghum, potatoes, livestock

Industry/mining: cement, agricultural products, small-scale beverages, soap, furniture, shoes, plastic goods, textiles, cigarettes

São Tomé and Príncipe

Agriculture: cocoa, coconuts, palm kernels, copra, cinnamon, pepper, coffee, bananas, papayas, beans, poultry, fish

Industry/mining: light construction, textiles, soap, beer, fish processing, timber

Senegal

Agriculture: peanuts, millet, corn, sorghum, rice, cotton, tomatoes, green vegetables, cattle, poultry, pigs, fish

Industry/mining: agricultural and fish processing, phosphate mining, fertilizer production, petroleum refining, construction materials

Seychelles

Agriculture: coconuts, cinnamon, vanilla, sweet potatoes, cassava (tapioca), bananas, broiler chickens, tuna fish

Industry/mining: fishing, tourism, processing of coconuts and vanilla, coir (coconut fiber) rope, boat building, printing, furniture, beverages

Sierra Leone

Agriculture: rice, coffee, cocoa, palm kernels, palm oil, peanuts, poultry, cattle, sheep, pigs, fish
Industry/mining: mining (diamonds), small-scale manufacturing (beverages, textiles, cigarettes, footwear), petroleum refining

Somalia

Agriculture: cattle, sheep, goats, bananas, sorghum, corn, coconuts, rice, sugarcane, mangoes, sesame seeds, beans, fish
Industry/mining: a few light industries, including sugar refining, textiles, petroleum refining (mostly shut down), wireless communication

South Africa

Agriculture: corn, wheat, sugarcane, fruits, vegetables, beef, poultry, mutton, wool, dairy products
Industry/mining: mining (world's largest producer of platinum, gold, chromium), automobile assembly, metalworking, machinery, textile, iron and steel, chemicals, fertilizer, foodstuffs

Sudan

Agriculture: cotton, groundnuts (peanuts), sorghum, millet, wheat, gum arabic, sugarcane, cassava (tapioca), mangos, papaya, bananas, sweet potatoes, sesame, sheep, livestock
Industry/mining: oil, cotton ginning, textiles, cement, edible oils, sugar, soap distilling, shoes,

petroleum refining, pharmaceuticals, armaments, automobile/light truck assembly

Swaziland

Agriculture: sugarcane, cotton, corn, tobacco, rice, citrus, pineapples, sorghum, peanuts, cattle, goats, sheep
Industry/mining: mining (coal), wood pulp, sugar, soft drink concentrates, textile and apparel

Tanzania

Agriculture: coffee, sisal, tea, cotton, pyrethrum (insecticide made from chrysanthemums), cashew nuts, tobacco, cloves, corn, wheat, cassava (tapioca), bananas, fruits, vegetables, cattle, sheep, goats
Industry/mining: agricultural processing (sugar, beer, cigarettes, sisal twine), diamond and gold mining, oil refining, shoes, cement, textiles, wood products, fertilizer, salt

Togo

Agriculture: coffee, cocoa, cotton, yams, cassava (tapioca), corn, beans, rice, millet, sorghum, livestock, fish
Industry/mining: phosphate mining, agricultural processing, cement, handicrafts, textiles, beverages

Tunisia

Agriculture: olives, olive oil, grain, dairy products, tomatoes, citrus fruit, beef, sugar beets, dates, almonds
Industry/mining: petroleum, mining (particularly phosphate

and iron ore), tourism, textiles, footwear, agribusiness, beverages

Uganda

Agriculture: coffee, tea, cotton, tobacco, cassava (tapioca), potatoes, corn, millet, pulses, beef, goat meat, milk, poultry, cut flowers
Industry/mining: sugar, brewing, tobacco, cotton textiles, cement

Western Sahara (claimed by Morocco)

Agriculture: fruits and vegetables (grown in the few oases), camels, sheep, goats (kept by nomads)
Industry/mining: phosphate mining, handicrafts

Zambia

Agriculture: corn, sorghum, rice, peanuts, sunflower seed, vegetables, flowers, tobacco, cotton, sugarcane, cassava (tapioca), cattle, goats, pigs, poultry, milk, eggs, hides, coffee
Industry/mining: copper mining and processing, construction, foodstuffs, beverages, chemicals, textiles, fertilizer, horticulture

Zimbabwe

Agriculture: corn, cotton, tobacco, wheat, coffee, sugarcane, peanuts, cattle, sheep, goats, pigs
Industry/mining: mining (coal, gold, copper, nickel, tin, clay, numerous metallic and nonmetallic ores), steel, wood products, cement, chemicals, fertilizer, clothing and footwear, foodstuffs, beverages

Source: CIA World Factbook, 2011

Africa is home to many diverse peoples and cultures. (Opposite) Masai warriors, wearing traditional costume, perform a battle dance. (Right) A Mauritanian woman poses with her family's goat.

4 The People

THE COMMON PERCEPTION is that Africa is socially and culturally homogeneous. Nothing could be further from the truth. Africa is an incredibly diverse continent: over 3,000 distinct ethnic groups, each with its own culture and traditions, call Africa home, and more than 800 languages are spoken there. Africans worship in churches, mosques, Hindu temples, and synagogues—and many still practice their ethnic group's traditional religion. While a majority of Africans are black, a significant number of them trace their roots to India, Europe, and the Arab world.

ARAB NORTH AFRICA

Most of the roughly 150 million people who live in North Africa, which includes the countries of Egypt, Libya, Tunisia, Algeria, Morocco, and

51

Mauritania, consider themselves to be Arabs, and virtually everyone in these countries speaks Arabic. As far back as 5,000 years ago, the *indigenous* inhabitants of North Africa included the ancient Egyptians and the Berbers, whose descendants still live in the mountains of Morocco, Algeria, and Tunisia. Prior to the Arab invasion in the seventh century, numerous other Mediterranean peoples had conquered and lived in North Africa, including the Phoenicians, Romans, and Greeks. The invading Arabs intermarried with the local population, and converted the majority of them to Islam. North Africa was later ruled by the Ottoman Turks and by European countries like France and Italy. Thus, today the average North African has a mixed ethnic heritage.

Although each of the North African countries has its own distinct characteristics and traditions, they all have a culture, language, and social framework that give them an Arab identity. And while they still regard themselves as African nations, their economies and their politics are more oriented

Women of the Comoros Islands wear *shiromanis*, long garments that blend African, Arab, and Persian designs. The culture of East Africa reflects a historical combination of influences from Arabia, Persia, and Southeast Asia over more than 10 centuries.

toward the Middle East and Europe than to the rest of Africa. Geography plays a powerful role in keeping the North African nations somewhat distinct: the vast and unwelcoming Sahara Desert separates North Africa from the rest of the continent. Prior to modern air transportation, it could take weeks of extremely dangerous travel to cross the Sahara. The only people who then called the Sahara home were the Tuareg, a nomadic group who can still be found in northern Mali.

SUB-SAHARAN AFRICA

The area south of the Sahara is known as sub-Saharan Africa. The vast majority of the people who live here are black, but their similarities end there. Sub-Saharan Africa is one of the most culturally diverse regions in the world. A single country may have a multitude of languages, artistic and musical styles, and social traditions.

The Amhara are the major ethnic group living in Ethiopia. They are predominantly farmers and herders living in rugged mountainous areas. According to Amhara tradition, the people originally migrated across the Red Sea from the Arabian Peninsula around 1000 B.C. The ancient language they speak, Amharic, is related to Arabic and Hebrew. Today, most Amharas are Christian and are members of the Ethiopian Orthodox Church.

The Ashanti are an ethnic group living primarily in central Ghana; they once were part of one of Africa's greatest empires. Although they are citizens of Ghana today, the Ashanti still recognize their king and practice their religion, which is based on belief in numerous spiritual and supernatural powers. The Ashanti are famous for their crafts and garments, in particular their carved wooden sculptures and a beautiful type of handwoven cloth known as *kente*.

The San (also known as Bushmen)—a name used for several related ethnic groups—are the oldest inhabitants of southern Africa, where they have lived for 20,000 years. The San, who are mostly hunter-gatherers, live in and around the Kalahari Desert, which covers parts of Botswana, South Africa, and Namibia. They speak several unique languages, which have clicking sounds not used in any other language.

The largest ethnic group in southern Africa is the Zulu, who migrated south from the Congo River region in the 17th and 18th centuries. The Zulu fought a fierce war against the British in 1879, ultimately losing and having to cede their lands to the colonial power. Today the Zulu make up a significant segment of South Africa's population.

The Fulani people have settlements throughout much of West Africa. They were traditionally a nomadic cattle-raising people, although today many have settled in the towns and villages of West African countries such as Mali, Niger, Nigeria, Burkina Faso, and Guinea. The Fulani were the first black Africans to convert to Islam, and they played a major role in spreading the religion throughout West Africa. Other major West African ethnic groups include the Wolof, the dominant group in Senegal; and the Dogon, who live in cliff dwellings in Mali and Burkina Faso and are known for their intricate wood-carvings. The Yoruba people, who live in Nigeria and Benin, have an elaborate religious system that includes the belief in over 400 gods. They tend to live mostly in Lagos, Nigeria, and other large cities. Yoruba artwork is renowned throughout the world among lovers of African art, and includes beautiful pottery, beadwork, masks, and metalwork.

For centuries, the plains of East Africa were populated by the Masai, who gained notoriety as warriors and cattle herders. Today, they are mainly settled in the cities and towns of Kenya and Tanzania. The traditional Masai religion taught that there was one god who lived in all things, but many Masai have converted to Christianity. The language of this group, called Maa, is spoken by over a million people in Kenya and Tanzania.

The Pygmy people are forest dwellers who live in a large area that encompasses the Democratic Republic of the Congo, the Republic of the Congo, Cameroon, Gabon, Central African Republic, Rwanda, Burundi, and Uganda. They demonstrate expert knowledge of the forest's plants and animals and survive by fishing; hunting antelopes, pigs, and monkeys; and gathering honey, yams, berries, and other edible plants. The Pygmies believe in a powerful spirit of the forest called Jengi.

RELIGIONS OF AFRICA

Many Africans still practice traditional, or indigenous, religions. These often include the worship of spirits and deceased ancestors, and the belief that all living things, including animals and plants, contain spirits. In a few countries, such as Togo, Mozambique, and Madagascar, indigenous religions remain the predominant belief system. Even in countries where one of the major world religions is well established, certain customs and practices from indigenous religions frequently find their way into church services and holiday celebrations.

The peoples of Arab North Africa are almost entirely Muslim, except for a small Christian community in Egypt, and very small Jewish communities in

QUICK FACTS: THE PEOPLE OF AFRICA

Total Population: 1,051,494,600
Algeria: 33,333,216
Angola: 15,941,000
Benin: 8,439,000
Botswana: 1,839,833
Burkina Faso: 13,228,000
Burundi: 7,548,000
Cameroon: 17,795,000
Cape Verde: 420,979
Central African Republic: 4,216,666
Chad: 10,146,000
Comoros: 798,000
Democratic Republic of the Congo: 71,712,867
Republic of the Congo: 4,012,809
Djibouti: 909,837
Egypt: 80,335,036
Equatorial Guinea: 504,000
Eritrea: 5,880,000

Ethiopia: 85,237,338
Gabon: 1,384,000
The Gambia: 1,517,000
Ghana: 23,000,000
Guinea: 9,402,000
Guinea-Bissau: 1,586,000
Ivory Coast: 17,654,843
Kenya: 34,707,817
Lesotho: 1,795,000
Liberia: 3,283,000
Libya: 6,036,914
Madagascar: 18,606,000
Malawi: 12,884,000
Mali: 13,518,000
Mauritania: 3,069,000
Mauritius: 1,219,220
Morocco: 35,757,175
Mozambique: 20,366,795
Namibia: 2,031,000

Morocco, Tunisia, and Egypt. Islam is also well established in West Africa and parts of East Africa. Over 80 percent of the people in Guinea, Mali, Mauritania, Senegal, and the Gambia are Muslim. Nigeria, Africa's most populous country, is around 50 percent Muslim. The East African countries of Ethiopia, Somalia, Djibouti, and the Comoros Islands are all predominantly Muslim.

Very few Muslims live in central and southern Africa, which is predominantly Christian. More than 75 percent of the people in Lesotho, Malawi,

Niger: 13,957,000
Nigeria: 154,729,000
Rwanda: 7,600,000
São Tomé and Príncipe: 157,000
Senegal: 11,685,000
Seychelles: 80,654
Sierra Leone: 6,144,562
Somalia: 9,832,017
South Africa: 47,432,000
South Sudan: 8,260,490
Sudan: 36,787,012
Swaziland: 1,032,000
Tanzania: 37,849, 133
Togo: 6,100,000
Tunisia: 10,102,000
Uganda: 27,616,000
Zambia: 14,668,000
Zimbabwe: 13,010,000

Religions: Various traditional indigenous religions; Islam predominant in the north and west; Christianity widespread in the south and east; Hindu minorities in southern Africa; small Jewish communities in North Africa and South Africa.
Languages: Arabic in North Africa; French in west and central Africa; English in parts of West Africa, widespread in East and South Africa; Portuguese in Angola and Mozambique; over 800 indigenous languages and dialects.
Population growth rate: 2.3%

All figures are 2011 estimates.
Sources: CIA World Fact Book; Population Reference Bureau.

Namibia, Rwanda, and South Africa follow Christianity. Other countries in which Christianity is the main religion include Angola, Burundi, the Democratic Republic of the Congo, Gabon, Kenya, and Uganda. Only 40 percent of Nigerians are Christian, though because the national population is so large, this segment is one of the largest Christian communities in Africa.

One African nation, the island country of Mauritius, has a majority Hindu population because of the large number of its citizens who are descendants of Indians. South Africa also has a substantial Hindu population and a small Jewish community.

AFRICAN MUSIC

Music is an extremely important aspect of life, society, and culture for just about every African ethnic group, in every African country. People sing and play instruments to celebrate religious holidays and important family events like weddings and funerals. In a part of the world where many people do not read or write, songs often became the principal means of communicating and passing down stories and traditions.

Like other cultural attributes, African music varies considerably from one ethnic group to another. Frequently, a musical style of one group will gain popularity with other groups—a strong argument that music is truly Africa's universal language. The Democratic Republic of the Congo is famous for its dance music. East African music is strongly influenced by Arab rhythms, and North African styles owe much to both Arab and Berber traditions. Algeria has developed a genre called *rai* that blends Arabic love songs and Berber folk music with influences from French, Moroccan, and Spanish music, as well as jazz and Jamaican reggae.

South African music is famous for its singing, especially the Zulu *a cappella* style. The country is also a major source of African jazz, reggae, and gospel music. West Africa has produced some of Africa's greatest musicians. Some of the contemporary musicians from the region, such as Alpha Blondy of the Ivory Coast and Youssou N'Dour of Senegal, have achieved global fame. Malian musicians have developed a type of folk music know as "desert blues."

AFRICAN LITERATURE

For most of Africa's history, stories and traditions were passed down either orally or through song. Very few people could read or write, and many of Africa's various languages did not even have a written form. But as more and more Africans learned to read and write in the 19th and 20th centuries, there was an explosion in African literature.

Much of African literature consists of traditional stories and legends, now permanently preserved in written form. But there is also a fascinating body of new literature by Africans that reflects their experiences with colonialism, their attempts to reconcile traditional values with modern values, and their daily struggle with the same issues that concern people everywhere.

One of Africa's best-known literary figures is the Nigerian writer Chinua Achebe. His works include *Things Fall Apart*, about the effects of British colonialism on Nigeria, and *No Longer at Ease*, about a young Nigerian who must readjust to life in his native country after living for a time in England. Camara Laye, a Guinean writer, is author of *The Dark Child*, a touching and fascinating account of his childhood in a Guinean village.

Four African authors have won literature's greatest honor, the Nobel Prize. Naguib Mahfouz, an Egyptian, penned several beautiful and powerful novels about daily life in a Cairo slum. Nadine Gordimer and J. M. Coetzee, both of whom are white South Africans, have written novels that deal with the immorality of the racist apartheid system in their country. Wole Soyinka, a Nigerian, is a writer of poetry, plays, and a highly acclaimed childhood memoir, *Ake: The Years of Childhood*.

Although most of Africa's population lives in rural areas, the continent is home to many large and cosmopolitan cities. (Opposite) Casablanca, the largest city in Morocco, is home to about 3.6 million people. (Right) Nairobi is the capital of Kenya and the largest city in East Africa.

5 The Cities

FOR MOST OF their history, Africans have lived in small towns and villages. During the precolonial and colonial eras, a few major cities developed—usually along the coasts, where trading was an important activity—but for the most part African society was rural. Today village life is still prevalent, but over the past 50 years the continent's cities have grown at a stunning rate.

The colonial powers that ruled most of Africa established their administrative headquarters in cities and also developed basic infrastructure. Upon achieving independence, the new African governments were eager to establish thriving capital cities, with the specific aim of solidifying central control over societies that were usually composed of many different ethnic groups. As life in rural areas became more difficult, young people began moving to the cities to seek jobs and educational opportunities. Rapid population growth also led to rapid urban growth, so that today Africa has some of the world's largest cities. Accompanying this growth have been many of the problems commonly associated with urban areas, including pollution, crime, and alienation.

ABIDJAN, IVORY COAST

With a population of over 5 million in 2012, Abidjan is one of the most modern cities in Africa. It is Ivory Coast's business and commercial center, and is also home to many government offices, although the country's official capital is Yamoussoukro. Abidjan boasts the largest port in West Africa, and its downtown area—known as "the Plateau"—has some of Africa's tallest skyscrapers.

ADDIS ABABA, ETHIOPIA

Addis Ababa has grown from a small village in the early 20th century to a sprawling city of over 3 million people, according to recent estimates. Ethiopia's capital has one of the largest open-air markets in Africa, a beautiful Christian cathedral built in 1896, and several fascinating museums. It is a poor city, and in recent years has been flooded with refugees fleeing ethnic violence in other parts of Ethiopia.

ANTANANARIVO, MADAGASCAR

This fascinating city, the capital of Madagascar, is home to about 1.4 million people, but seems as crowded, bustling, and polluted as much larger African cities. Antananarivo is filled with street markets and vendors selling all kinds of wares. As a country with some of the world's most unique wildlife, it is fitting that the capital's zoo features such a rare selection of animals.

CAIRO, EGYPT

Egypt's capital has a 2012 population of about 6.8 million people, with another 10 million living in its suburbs. Cairo is the largest city in Africa and the 11th-largest metropolitan area in the world. It is also one of the most important cities in the Arab world, as it is home to the headquarters of the League of Arab States and to Al-Azhar University, one of the oldest and most renowned centers of Islamic learning. Cairo is a teeming, bustling city, filled with historic buildings and the famous Egyptian Museum, which has the world's largest collection of ancient Egyptian mummies.

CAPE TOWN, SOUTH AFRICA

With over 3.5 million people, Cape Town is South Africa's second-largest city. Located on the sea, with soaring mountains as a backdrop and the famed

The Sultan Hassan Mosque is located in Cairo, Egypt. This ancient city is one of the most populous cities in the world.

Cape of Good Hope just a short distance away, the city boasts an impressive natural setting. Cape Town is home to one of South Africa's principal universities and has a large student population. It is also the scene of several annual music festivals and other cultural celebrations.

CASABLANCA, MOROCCO

Casablanca, a port city of about 3.6 million people, is the largest city in Morocco and is the country's industrial and business center (the capital of Morocco is Rabat). It is a cosmopolitan city with a long history of dealing with various foreign countries. The most stunning feature of Casablanca is the massive Hassan II Mosque, one of the largest Islamic places of worship in the world. The mosque can accommodate 105,000 people.

A panoramic view of Cape Town, South Africa. The first settlement on this site was established in 1652 by the Dutch East India Company as a stopping point for ships trading between Europe and Indonesia. In 1806 the British took permanent control over the colony and established their administrative headquarters at Cape Town.

DAKAR, SENEGAL

Dakar, a crowded and lively port city of 2.45 million people, is the capital of Senegal and a center of both traditional and modern African music. Central Dakar is located on a narrow peninsula that juts out into the Atlantic Ocean. It features some beautiful colonial French architecture and is close to a number of warm, sunny beaches.

DAR ES SALAAM, TANZANIA

Tanzania's largest city (home to around 2.5 million people) is also one of Africa's cleanest and safest urban areas. A busy port, Dar es Salaam (in Arabic, "haven of peace") has tree-lined streets and a colorful open-air central market. Located south of the city are beautiful beaches with palm trees and white sand.

JOHANNESBURG, SOUTH AFRICA

With over 5 million people, Johannesburg ("Jo'burg" to its residents) is the largest and most important city in South Africa. Most of South Africa's major gold and diamond companies are based in Johannesburg, as are the country's banks and financial institutions. It is home to some of South Africa's richest citizens, who live in walled and guarded compounds, and to some of its poorest, who live in dismal *shantytowns*.

KAMPALA, UGANDA

Uganda's capital and largest city (around 1.7 million people) suffered greatly during decades of civil war, but was largely rebuilt as a modern city, with nice shops, restaurants, and hotels. Kampala is built on seven hills, and each area of the city has a unique feel. Unlike many African cities, Kampala is regarded as safe, and is home to several international aid organizations.

KINSHASA, DEMOCRATIC REPUBLIC OF THE CONGO

Kinshasa, Africa's third-largest metropolitan area, is a huge and sprawling city with a population of about 10 million. Kinshasa sits along the Congo River, which is a major conduit for trade. It is crowded and at times has been the scene of ethnic violence and crime. Directly across the river is Brazzaville, the capital city of the Republic of Congo, itself a metropolis of well over 1.2 million people.

LAGOS, NIGERIA

Lagos is a huge metropolitan area of more than 12 million people, and it is growing rapidly. It is estimated to be the seventh-fastest growing city in the world, and its population is projected to reach 25 million by 2020. As a result of the rapid growth many residents live in dilapidated shantytowns and lack basic services like water and electricity. Lagos is a busy port and the business center of Nigeria, but has also developed a terrible reputation for crime and overcrowded conditions.

MAPUTO, MOZAMBIQUE

Maputo was once regarded as one of the most beautiful cities in the world, but after a long war of independence against Portugal (1964–1974), followed by a devastating civil war (1977–1992), it has shown some wear. Nevertheless, Maputo still has some stunning colonial-era architecture, built in the Portuguese style, and a dynamic open-air market in the city center. With about 1.8 million people, it does not have the crowded feeling of many African cities.

NAIROBI, KENYA

Nairobi, Kenya's capital, is the largest city in East Africa. Its residents—numbering about 3.1 million—live in a busy, modern, and cosmopolitan city home to the very rich, the extremely destitute, and everyone in between. In recent years, Nairobi has had a serious crime problem, but it still attracts businesspeople and tourists from throughout the world.

MAPS AND FLAGS

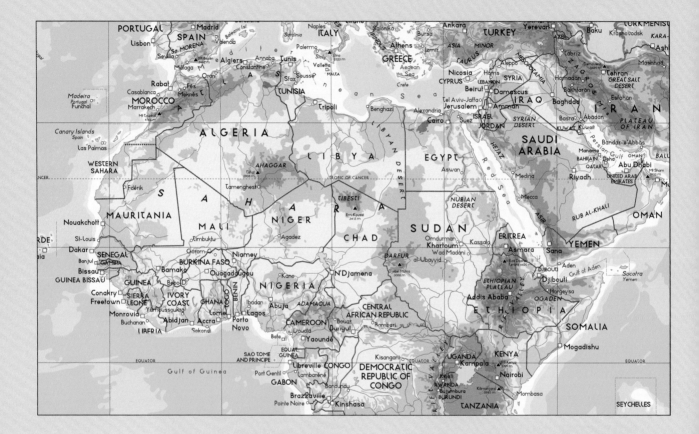

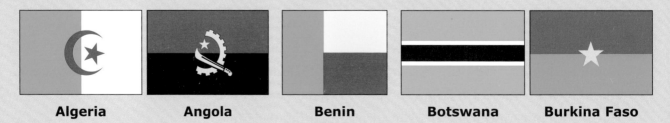

Algeria   **Angola**   **Benin**   **Botswana**   **Burkina Faso**

Burundi

Cameroon

Cape Verde

Central African Republic

Chad

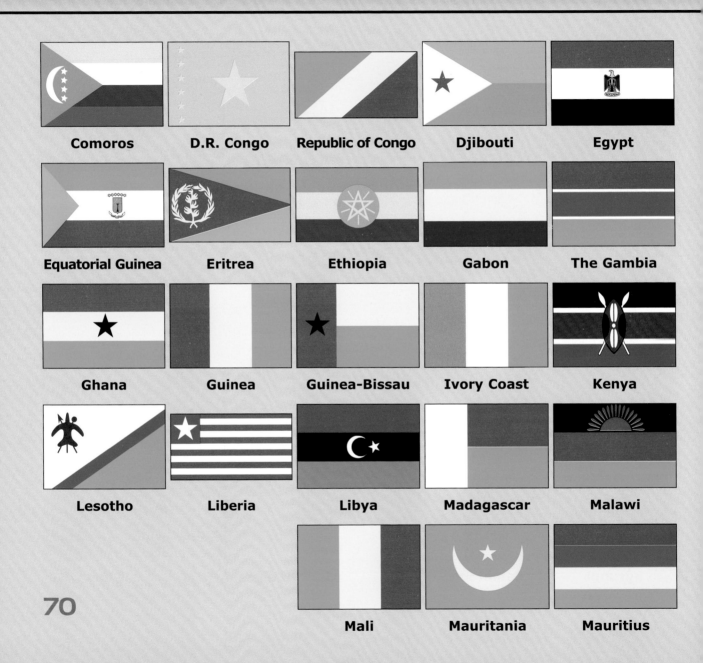

Comoros   D.R. Congo   Republic of Congo   Djibouti   Egypt

Equatorial Guinea   Eritrea   Ethiopia   Gabon   The Gambia

Ghana   Guinea   Guinea-Bissau   Ivory Coast   Kenya

Lesotho   Liberia   Libya   Madagascar   Malawi

Mali   Mauritania   Mauritius

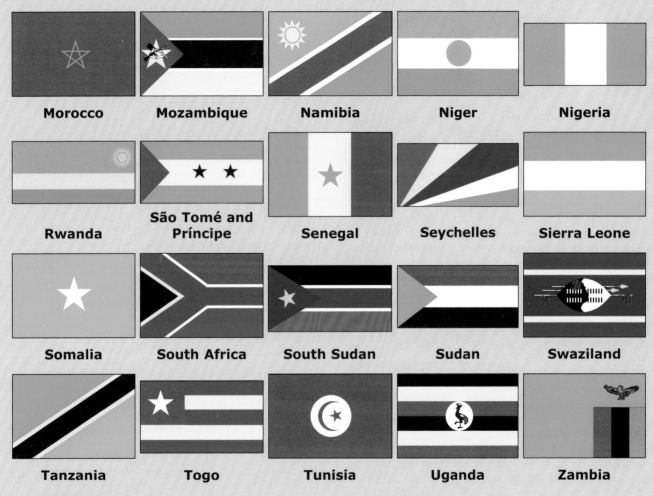

Morocco

Mozambique

Namibia

Niger

Nigeria

Rwanda

São Tomé and Príncipe

Senegal

Seychelles

Sierra Leone

Somalia

South Africa

South Sudan

Sudan

Swaziland

Tanzania

Togo

Tunisia

Uganda

Zambia

Zimbabwe

A CALENDAR OF AFRICAN FESTIVALS

Festivals and celebrations are a major part of life in Africa. Every ethnic group, as well as every country, has its own particular celebrations and holidays. Other celebrations are common to many parts of this vast continent. Below is a sampling of some of Africa's most important festivals.

January

New Year's Day is a holiday in many African countries, even those that do not follow the Western calendar. January 1 also is Independence Day in Sudan. Epiphany, a Christian holiday celebrating the baptism of Christ, is observed by Christian communities throughout the continent. In Ethiopia, Epiphany is known as Timkat, and is one of the most important celebrations of the Ethiopian Orthodox Church. In early January, Mali celebrates the annual Festival du Desert (Festival of the Desert), an international celebration of music and dancing held in Timbuktu. In Mauritius, which has a large Chinese community, the Chinese New Year is held on January 22.

February

Africa's largest annual film festival, the Fespaco Film Festival, is held in late February in Ouagadougou, Burkina Faso. In the Muslim areas of Nigeria, the annual Durbar Festival commemorates the glories of the former Muslim emirate of northern Nigeria. On the island of Zanzibar (part of Tanzania), the annual Swahili Music and Culture Festival is held on a three-day weekend in mid-February. It features Swahili music, theater, and dance. In Egypt, the Abu Simbel Festival, held on February 22 and December 22 at the ancient temple of the same name, is celebrated on the two days of the year that the sun shines directly upon the temple's shrine.

March

March 20 is Tunisia's Independence Day. The annual Carnaval de Bouaké in Ivory Coast has become one of Africa's largest festivities. It is an opportunity for the residents of Bouaké to show off their city and its culture. The carnival includes musical performances, culinary events, and an agricultural fair. The Kilimanjaro Marathon is held every March in Tanzania, attracting runners from around the world.

April

April 4 is Senegal's Independence Day. April 24, Freedom Day, is a major holiday in South Africa. In Mali, the Fete des Masques is a celebration of the mask-making tradition of the country's Dogon people.

May

Like much of the world, many African countries celebrate Labor Day as a public holiday on May 1. Mawlid al-Nabiy, the commemoration of the birthday of the prophet Muhammad, is a Muslim holiday celebrated by prayer and often a procession to the local mosque. The Aboakyer Festival, held in the villages of central Ghana, celebrates the migration of the Wineba people from Sudan to Ghana. The South Sinai Camel Festival in Egypt features camel races.

June

The annual Festival of the Dhow Countries, held in Zanzibar, celebrates the culture of the Muslim seafarers of the Indian Ocean. The World Festival of Sacred Music, held each year in Fez, Morocco, features diverse religious musical performances from around the world.

July

Independence Day is celebrated in Somalia, Burundi, and Rwanda on July 1, in Malawi on July 6, in the Republic of Southern Sudan on July 9, and in Liberia on July 26. Egyptians celebrate Revolution Day on July 23. The Panafest is a celebration of African performing arts held in Ghana.

72

A CALENDAR OF AFRICAN FESTIVALS

August

August 1 is **National Day** in Benin, and August 11 is **Independence Day** in Chad. The **Homowo Festival** is an annual harvest celebration in Ghana. The **International Camel Derby and Festival**, held in Kenya, features a long camel race as well as music and other events.

September

The **Imilchil Wedding Festival** in Morocco is a unique event in which young men and women gather in the village of Imilchil and brides choose their grooms. The **Hermanus Whale Festival** in South Africa is a celebration of nature featuring whale-watching, music, food, and performances.

October

October 1 is **Independence Day** in Nigeria and October 2 in Guinea. **Fete de l'Abissa** is a weeklong carnival held in the former colonial capital and beach resort of Grand Bassam in Ivory Coast. The **Cairo Film Festival** is the most important film event in the Arab world.

November

Among Christian communities, November 1 is **All Saints' Day**, a holiday honoring all of the church's saints. The village of Man in Ivory Coast is the scene of the annual **Fetes des Masques** (Festival of Masks). The **Mombasa Carnival**, in Kenya, features parades with floats representing each of Kenya's many cultural influences.

December

The **Crossing of the Cattle** is an important holiday in Mali, honoring the cattle herders who spend most of the year seeking grazing grounds. **Incwala**, a holiday celebrated in Swaziland, kicks off the harvest season with religious and family celebrations. Africa's Christians celebrate **Christmas Day** on December 25 with church services and family gatherings. It also is a national holiday in many countries.

Other Religious Celebrations

African Muslims and Christians observe a number of important holy days related to their religions. Some of these, such as Christmas, are on particular days each year. However, many other major celebrations are held according to a lunar calendar, in which the months correspond to the phases of the moon. A lunar month is shorter than a typical month of the Western calendar. Therefore, the festival dates vary from year to year. Other celebrations are observed seasonally.

Ramadan is a month-long Muslim holiday during which time devout Muslims fast and pray throughout the daylight hours. It is the holiest period in Islam. As soon as the sun goes down, families and friends gather in homes for a meal marking the end of the fasting day. At the end of Ramadan, Muslims celebrate a major holiday called **Eid al-Fitr** (Festival of the Breaking of the Fast). This is a joyous time characterized by feasts and the exchange of gifts.

Eid al-Adha (Feast of Sacrifice) takes place in the last month of the Muslim calendar during the hajj period, when Muslims make a pilgrimage to Mecca. The holiday honors the prophet Abraham, who was willing to sacrifice his own son to Allah. Each of these holidays is celebrated with a feast. On Eid al-Adha, families traditionally eat a third of the feast and donate the rest to the poor.

The major Christian festivals on the lunar cycle involve the suffering and death of Jesus Christ. **Ash Wednesday** marks the start of a period of self-sacrifice called **Lent**, which lasts for 40 days. The final eight days of Lent, which include **Palm Sunday**, **Holy Thursday**, **Good Friday**, and **Easter**, are known as **Holy Week**.

73

RECIPES

Moroccan Chicken Tagine with Honey and Apricots

2 chickens, cut up
2 large yellow onions
2 sticks of butter
1/2 tsp. turmeric
1 tsp. black pepper
2 cinnamon sticks
1 lb. dried apricots
8 Tbsp. honey, or more to taste
2 tsp. ground cinnamon
1/2 cup peeled almonds
1 Tbsp. sesame seeds
Olive oil

Directions:

1. Melt the butter in a large pot. Fry the onions until soft, then add the chicken pieces, salt, pepper, turmeric, and cinnamon sticks. Add enough water to cover the chicken. Bring to a boil, then reduce heat and simmer until chicken is done.
2. Remove chicken from pot. Add the apricots and simmer for about 15 minutes. Add the ground cinnamon and honey, stirring constantly.
3. Meanwhile, sauté the almonds in olive oil until lightly browned. Drain out most of the oil and add the sesame seeds; sauté for about one minute until seeds are toasted.
4. Return the chicken to the pot and bring to a simmer. Serve the chicken on top of rice or couscous, with almonds and toasted sesame seeds on top.

Zimbabwean Peanut Butter Stew

2 medium onions, chopped
2 Tbsp. butter
2 cloves garlic, crushed
1 tsp. salt
1/2 tsp. black pepper
1/2 tsp. cayenne pepper
2 green peppers, chopped
1 chicken, cut into pieces
1 large can tomatoes (or about 4 fresh tomatoes)
6 Tbsp. creamy peanut butter
1/2 lb. of spinach

Directions:

1. In a large stew pot, sauté onions in butter until soft and golden brown. Add garlic, salt, black pepper, and cayenne pepper.
2. Stir for a few minutes, then add chopped green peppers and chicken pieces.
3. When the chicken pieces are browned on all sides, mash tomatoes with a fork and mix them into the stew, along with about 2 cups of water. Reduce heat and simmer for 5 to 10 minutes.
4. Add a few spoonfuls of the hot broth to the peanut butter and stir until soft; add half of the peanut butter to the stew pot. Simmer until the chicken is cooked through.
5. In a separate pot, boil spinach for 2 or 3 minutes until tender. Drain and toss with the remainder of the peanut butter. Serve stew and greens together.

Ghanaian *Kelewele* (Fried Bananas)

2 or 3 ripe but firm bananas (better to use plantains, if available)
2 1/2 Tbsp. of cooking oil
1 tsp. cayenne pepper
1 medium onion, chopped
3 cloves of garlic, minced
1 small piece of fresh ginger, minced (or 1 tsp. ground ginger)
1 tsp. salt

Directions:
1. Mix the red pepper, onion, garlic, ginger, and salt in a small bowl. Add 1 Tbsp. of oil.
2. Peel the bananas and slice into 1/2-inch thick pieces. Pour the spice mixture over the bananas, and refrigerate for one hour.
3. Heat the remaining oil in a skillet over medium heat. When hot, add the bananas in a single layer; brown on each side.

The bananas can be served as dessert or with dinner as a side dish.

Tanzanian Fruit Pie

9-inch frozen piecrust
1 1/2 cups of papaya, guava, or apricot nectar
4 Tbsp. cornstarch
4 Tbsp. lemon juice
8 Tbsp. sugar
1/2 tsp. salt
2 cups diced fresh fruits, such as papaya, pineapple, oranges, guava, or melon (can use any combination)
1 cup heavy cream
1/2 cup shredded coconut
1/2 cup peanuts

Directions:
1. Bake piecrust according to package directions.
2. In a saucepan, bring the fruit nectar to a boil.
3. Dissolve 4 Tbsp. of cornstarch in 4 Tbsp. of lemon juice; add 4 Tbsp. of sugar and 1/2 tsp. of salt. Mix with the nectar and stir until clear.
4. Remove from heat, add diced fruit and let mixture cool to room temperature.
5. Pour fruit mixture into pie shell and chill in refrigerator.
6. Mix 1 cup of heavy cream with 4 Tbsp. of sugar, then spread on top of pie.
7. Sprinkle with coconut and peanuts.

GLOSSARY

a cappella—a musical form in which a choir sings without being accompanied by musical instruments.

anthropologist—a person who studies ethnic groups and cultures.

apartheid—a policy of racial segregation.

archaeologist—a person who studies the ruins and artifacts of past societies.

authoritarian—having a style of government in which all power is concentrated in one or a few leaders.

charismatic—attracting great popularity or loyalty.

cold war—the period of intense rivalry, but not actual warfare, between the United States and the Soviet Union from 1945 to 1991.

coup—the act of overthrowing a government, usually through military or violent means.

ecosystem—a community of plants and animals in a particular environment or area.

entrepreneurial—organizing, managing, and assuming the risks of a business or enterprise.

estuary—the wide lower course of a river where the tide flows in.

free market—an economic system in which businesses operate with limited or no government control.

genocide—the deliberate, systematic destruction of a racial, political, or cultural group.

gross domestic product (GDP)—the total value of all goods and services produced by a country in a given year.

indigenous—produced, growing, living, or occurring naturally in a particular region or environment.

isthmus—a narrow strip of land connecting two larger land areas.

nomadic—roaming from place to place.

oases—areas of the desert that receive water from an underground spring and can support plant and animal life.

papyrus—paper made from a type of grass that was used by the ancient Egyptians.

petrochemical—a chemical product made from oil.

pharmaceutical—a drug or medicine.

poacher—a person who illegally kills animals in the wild.

savanna—a flat grassland in a tropical or subtropical region.

scourge—something that causes widespread pain or illness.

shantytown—a poor and crowded section of a city consisting of very poor-quality housing.

socialist—relating to an economic system in which the government owns and operates production facilities.

subsistence—the condition of providing just enough food to support life.

PROJECT AND REPORT IDEAS

Maps

Draw or print from the Internet a blank map of Africa. Research the various African empires that ruled before colonialism. Label each empire on the map and shade the area that each controlled in a different color. Note important cities, such as Djenne and Timbuktu.

Draw or print from the Internet a blank map of Africa. Using a different color for each European power, denote each one's colonial holdings in Africa. Indicate which parts of Africa were not under colonial control.

Reports

Write a brief biography of one of Africa's great independence leaders, perhaps using a colorful poster. Possibilities include Léopold Senghor of Senegal; Kwame Nkrumah of Ghana; Julius Neyere of Tanzania; Jomo Kenyatta of Kenya; or Nelson Mandela of South Africa.

Research one of the recent or ongoing ethnic conflicts or civil wars in Africa (possibilities include the fighting in Sudan, Liberia, Sierra Leone, and Rwanda). In a one-page essay, describe which groups were in conflict and why. If the conflict was brought to an end, explain how.

Write a brief paper on the former apartheid system in South Africa. How did the black South Africans' struggle for independence resemble the civil rights movement in the United States? How was it different? What caused the apartheid system to be abolished? What is the current situation between blacks and whites in South Africa?

PROJECT AND REPORT IDEAS

Presentation

Listen to and read about the different African styles of music from various countries. Give a short oral presentation to the class covering each type of music you have researched. Be sure to answer the following questions: How are the various musical types similar? How are they different? What kinds of instruments are used in African music?

Creative Project

Using papier-mâché or pieces of cardboard, construct a traditional African mask. Do research in your library or on the Internet to find pictures of African masks. Learn the story behind the mask you have chosen to make and share it with the class.

CHRONOLOGY

5 million to 2.5 million B.C.	Fossils, rocks, and ancient skeletal remains indicate early human life in the Great Rift Valley of East Africa.
600,000–200,000	Evidence suggests that hunter-gatherer communities are established in Africa.
6000–4000	Societies emerge in areas along the Nile, Niger, and Congo Rivers.
ca. 4500	Ancient Egyptians develop first known written language and construct pyramids.
4000–1000	Ancient Egypt rises to its peak of power and influence.
ca. 1000–800	Bantu people migrate from West Africa to southern Africa.
500	Ancient Nok culture thrives in central Nigeria.
ca. A.D. 120	The Roman Empire finishes securing control of the North African coast.
4th century	The Aksum Empire converts to Christianity.
639–641	Muslim Arab armies conquer Egypt.
700–800	Islam sweeps across North Africa.
800–1100	The trans-Sahara gold trade flourishes in the Sahel region.
1000–1400	Yoruban culture flourishes in West Africa, producing terra-cotta and bronze artwork.
13th century	The Mali Empire rises to power.
ca. 1400	Mali Empire goes into decline; Swahili cities flourish on East African coast.
1441	The European slave trade begins with a shipment of slaves from West Africa to Portugal.
1480s	Europeans arrive on the east coast of Africa.
Late 15th century	The Kongo Kingdom flourishes on the Congo River.
1562	Britain begins trading slaves in Africa.
1570	The Portuguese establish a colony in Angola.
1652	The Dutch establish a colony at the Cape of Good Hope, in southern Africa.
1700–1717	The Ashanti Empire rises to power in Ghana.
18th century	The Atlantic slave trade reaches its height; millions of Africans are shipped to the Americas.
1884–85	Berlin Conference divides Africa among European powers.
1888	Brazil becomes the last major international power to abolish the slave trade.
1912	The African National Congress (ANC) is founded in South Africa to defend the rights of blacks under white rule.
1922	Egypt becomes constitutional monarchy, officially independent of Britain.
1935	Italy invades Ethiopia, but Italian troops are defeated in 1944.

80

1954	Gamal Abdel Nasser seizes power in Egypt; British troops are removed from Egypt and Nasser is elected Egypt's first president; Algerian war of independence begins.
1956	Morocco and Tunisia become independent.
1957	Ghana becomes independent.
1958	South Africa officially gains independence from Great Britain.
1960	Seventeen African countries gain independence—Nigeria, Senegal, Mali, Belgian Congo, French Congo, Ivory Coast, Upper Volta (now Burkina Faso), Cameroon, Somalia, Dahomey (Benin), Mauritania, Madagascar, Niger, Chad, Togo, Gabon, and the Central African Republic.
1962	Algeria wins independence from France after eight years of bloody fighting.
1963	The Organization of African Unity (OAU) is formed.
1967–70	Biafran civil war is fought in Nigeria.
1971	Idi Amin assumes power in Uganda, beginning one of the most repressive regimes in Africa.
1975	Cape Verde, Guinea-Bissau, Mozambique, and Angola gain independence from Portugal.
1980	Rhodesia gains independence and majority rule; changes its name to Zimbabwe.
1989	Civil war breaks out in Liberia, continues through 2003.
1990	Black South African leader Nelson Mandela is released from prison after serving 27 years.
1991	The apartheid system is abolished in South Africa; the country prepares for multiracial elections.
1994	At least 500,000 Tutsi civilians are massacred by Hutu vigilantes in Rwanda; Nelson Mandela is inaugurated president of South Africa.
1999	After years of military rule, Nigeria holds democratic elections; Thabo Mbeki replaces Mandela as South Africa's president.
2000	Fighting is halted over the Eritrea-Ethiopian border dispute, though it remains unresolved.
2004	Sudanese government and rebel leaders hold peace talks to end decades of civil war.
2008	The International Criminal Court accuses Sudan's President, Omar al-Bashir, of crimes against humanity committed in the Darfur region.
2011	Long-established governments are overthrown in Tunisia, Egypt, and Libya; dictator Muammar Gaddafi is captured by rebel forces and killed in October.
2012	The viral video *Kony 2012* is released in March, drawing international attention to Ugandan warlord Joseph Kony of the Lord's Resistance Army.

FURTHER READING/INTERNET RESOURCES

Akokpari, John, et al. *The African Union and Its Institutions*. Johannesburg: Jacana Media, 2009.

Friedenthal, Lora, and Dorothy Kavanaugh. *Religions of Africa*. Philadelphia: Mason Crest, 2007.

Gilbert, Erik. *Africa in World History*. 3rd ed. Upper Saddle River, N.J.: Prentice Hall, 2011.

Meredith, Martin. *The Fate of Africa: A History of the Continent Since Independence*. New York: Public Affairs, 2011.

Ross, Robert. *A Concise History of South Africa*. 2nd ed. New York: Cambridge University Press, 2008.

History and Geography

http://www.geographia.com/indx06.htm
http://www.bbc.co.uk/worldservice/africa/features/storyofafrica
http://www.mnh.si.edu/africanvoices
http://www.pbs.org/wonders

Economic and Political Information

http://www.afrol.com
http://www.africaaction.org
http://www.undp.org/rba
http://www.afbis.com

Culture and Festivals

http://www.nmafa.si.edu
http://www.africanceremonies.com
http://digicoll.library.wisc.edu/AfricaFocus/
http://www.pbs.org/wnet/africa
http://www.african.net

African Union
P.O. Box 3243
Roosevelt Street (Old Airport Area)
W21K19
Addis Ababa
Ethiopia
Tel: (+251) 1 51 77 00
Fax: (+251) 1 51 78 44
Web site: http://www.africa-union.org

Global Coalition for Africa
1919 Pennsylvania Avenue, NW, Suite 550
Washington, DC 20006
Tel.: (202) 458-4338/4272
Fax: (202) 522-3259

Africare
Africare House
440 R Street, NW
Washington, DC 20001-1935
Tel.: (202) 462-3614
Fax: (202) 387-1034
Web site: http://www.africare.org

TransAfrica Forum
1426 21st Street, NW
Second Floor
Washington, DC 20036
Tel: (202) 223-1960
Fax: (202) 223-1966
Web site: http://www.transafricaforum.org

The Corporate Council on Africa
1100 17th Street, NW, Suite 1100
Washington, DC 20036
Tel: (202) 835-1115
Fax: (202) 835-1117
Web site: http://www.africacncl.org

INDEX

Numbers in ***bold italic*** refer to captions.

INDEX

PICTURE CREDITS

CONTRIBUTORS

Professor Robert I. Rotberg is Director of the Program on Intrastate Conflict and Conflict Resolution at the Kennedy School, Harvard University, and President of the World Peace Foundation. He is the author of a number of books and articles on Africa, including *A Political History of Tropical Africa* and *Ending Autocracy, Enabling Democracy: The Tribulations of Southern Africa*.

William Mark Habeeb is a professor and international affairs consultant in Washington, D.C. He specializes in Middle East politics and conflict resolution. He has written widely on such topics as international negotiation, the politics and culture of North African states, and the Arab-Israeli conflict. He received his PhD in international relations from the Johns Hopkins University School of Advanced International Studies.